P9-CSH-275

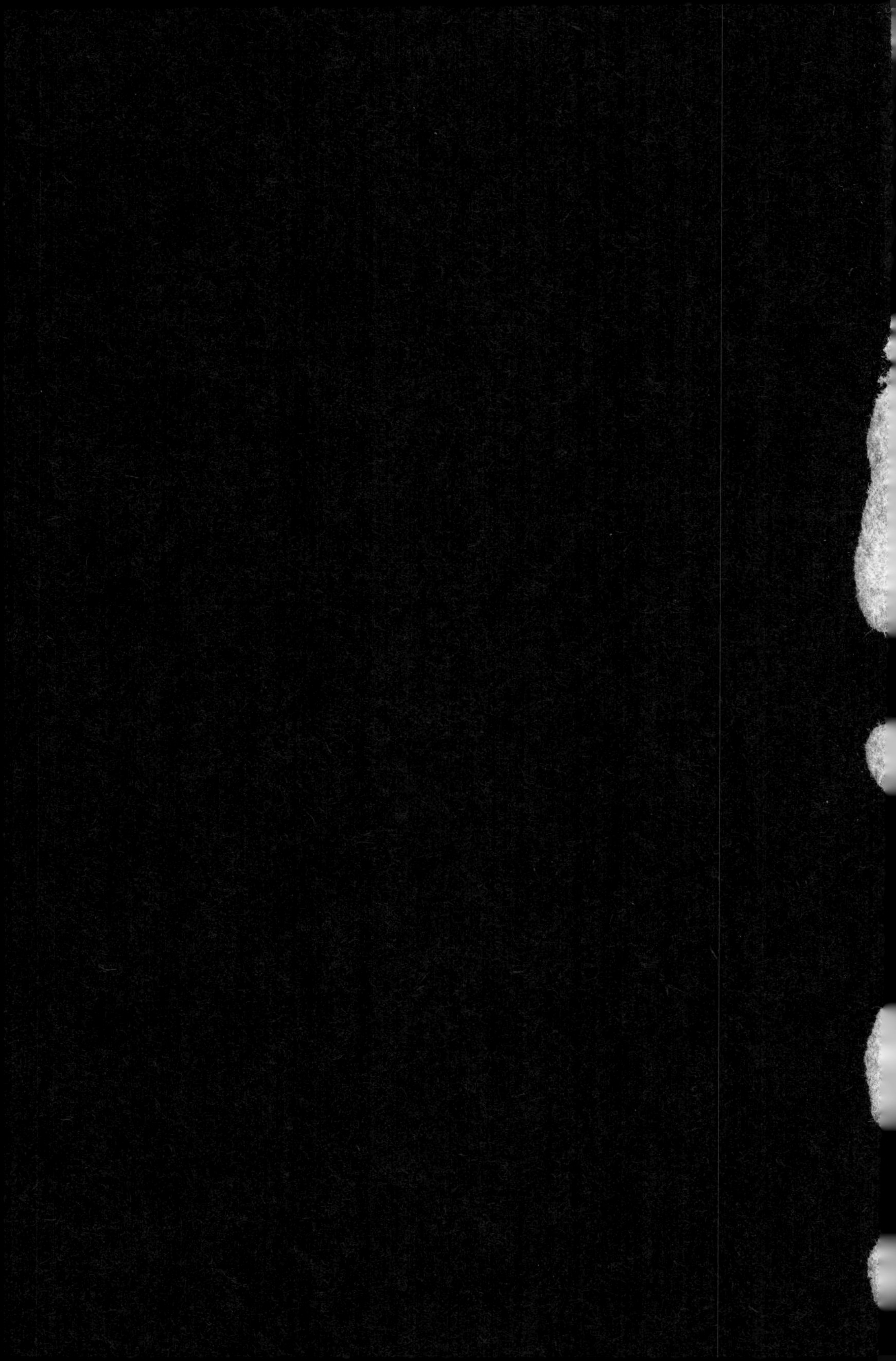

# PSYCHOANALYTIC OBJECT RELATIONS THERAPY

## COMMENTARY

"Althea Horner is a contemporary master of the theory and practice of modern psychoanalytic psychotherapy. Her past vital contributions to the field are widely acknowledged. Her wisdom and overview of a complex field like ours permit her to lead us directly to the heart of one important issue after another. When done, we know that we have covered with acute insight every vital area within the field. On our way we are introduced to the key classic and modern references vital to each and every subject. Thus, Althea Horner's book will prove to be valuable not only as a tool for the beginning therapist, but also as a reference and a well-structured and intelligent overview for the experienced and learned therapist as well."

—Marlin Brenner, Ph.D.

"Dr. Horner has produced a work that is an excellent blend of erudition, practical advice, and human warmth so often needed to offset the novice's tendency to either plunge into technical/theoretical 'purity' or foreswear all wisdom garnered by elders and only do what 'feels loving or empathic,' both at the patient's expense. I prescribe Dr. Horner for both new and experienced psychotherapists whose work is tending toward these two common means of dealing with our 'impossible profession.'"

—William Rickles, M.D.

"Althea Horner's outstanding contribution lies in her ability to avoid the traps of dogma and rigidity while maintaining discipline in theory and practical comprehension. The essential value of *Psychoanalytic Object Relations Therapy*, for the mental health practitioner, is Dr. Horner's lucid presentation of object relations theory and the translation of that theory into a practical object relations treatment approach."

—Seymour Coopersmith, Ed.D.

"Within these covers, any psychotherapy student, educator/supervisor, and practitioner, from the most embryonic to the most mature, will find material that will increase his/her capacity to listen, to feel, to intuit, and to synthesize what is going on within the dynamic therapeutic context."

—L. Arnold Wyse, M.D.

# PSYCHOANALYTIC OBJECT RELATIONS THERAPY

ALTHEA J. HORNER, Ph.D.

**JASON ARONSON INC.**
*Northvale, New Jersey*
*London*

Production Editor: *Judith D. Cohen*
Editorial Director: *Muriel Jorgensen*

This book was set in 12/15 Times Roman
by Lind Graphics of Upper Saddle River, New Jersey,
and printed and bound by Haddon Craftsmen of Scranton, Pennsylvania.



10 9 8 7 6 5 4 3 2 1



**Library of Congress Cataloging-in-Publication Data**

Horner, Althea J.
Psychoanalytic object relations therapy / Althea J. Horner.
p. cm.
Includes bibliographical references and index.
ISBN 0-87668-534-3
1. Object relations (Psychoanalysis) 2. Psychotherapy.
I. Title.
RC489.025H67 1991
616.89'17—dc20 91-3132

Manufactured in the United States of America. Jason Aronson Inc. offers books and cassettes. For information and catalog write to Jason Aronson Inc., 230 Livingston Street, Northvale, New Jersey 07647.

To the memory of
Edward N. Horner, M.D. –
*paterfamilias* and friend

# Contents

## Part II: Basic Concepts 57

# Preface

This book is written with the beginning psychodynamically oriented therapist in mind. Generally he or she is thrust into the role of therapist in graduate training with a confusing array of ideas, theories, and constructs. It is said that it takes 10 years to make a seasoned therapist, an indication of the significance of "hands on" experience in the process. It is hoped that this book will make it possible to begin that journey with a minimum of conceptual confusion and a greater sense of confidence.

The references at the end of this book serve as a ready guide through the literature for the reader who is motivated to broaden this introductory learning experience. In addition, the syllabus section offers a course of readings for the therapist who wishes to undertake further study on his or her own. Peer study groups, a stimulating approach to continuing education, may also find the references and syllabus a useful guide for their curriculum.

# Part I

# What Is Psychoanalytic Object Relations Therapy?

# CHAPTER 1

# Psychoanalytic Object Relations Therapy Defined

Psychoanalytic therapy is the approach to psychotherapy that is based on psychoanalytic developmental and clinical theory. This body of theory, beginning with Freud, has evolved over the past century, particularly over the past 25–30 years, and continues to evolve. Psychoanalytic therapy may or may not use the same specific techniques associated with psychoanalysis, such as the use of the couch or a requirement of four to five sessions a week. Cooper (1990) notes that "the traditional attempt to define psychoanalysis by a number [of sessions] and a technique rather than by a process trivializes analysis. The differences between psychoanalysis and psychotherapy are quite blurred . . ." (p. 189). He predicts that American psychoanalysis will increasingly concern itself with psychotherapy, and already we see psychoanalytic institutes offering a certificate in psychodynamic psychotherapy.

Psychoanalytic *object relations* therapy integrates concepts from a particular way of understanding human psychic development and organization, behavior, and interpersonal relationships, that being object relations theory. In the next chapter, this theory will be discussed in greater detail. Its usefulness is underscored by psychotherapy outcome studies that clearly indicate the correspondence of good outcome with a focus on the core relationship conflicts in treatment. These core conflicts are a manifestation of the inner psychic structure referred to as *object relations.* Derived from the earliest interpersonal matrix within which the psyche evolves, the inner object relations setup also functions as a prototype for here-and-now interpersonal relationships. Pathology of object relations—that is, pathology of the organization and structure of the psyche—becomes manifest in disturbed interpersonal relationships.

The basic principles or concepts common to both psychoanalysis and psychoanalytic therapy are (1) the existence of an unconscious mind that participates in human motivation and behavior to a greater or lesser degree—from an object relations perspective, this unconscious is organized in a particular way with object relations structure comprising the major organizing principle; (2) the existence of intrapsychic conflict that creates anxiety and the elaboration of defenses against that anxiety—structural pathology in object relations terms is considered alongside conflict as the etiology of symptoms; (3) a hierarchical development that, from the start, takes place in predictable stages and phases and that evolves in a manner resulting in the adult character structure—these stages vary from one theoretical orientation to another, for example, instinct theory with oral, anal, phallic, and genital stages is contrasted with the hierarchical stages of object relations development; (4) the possibility of regression to earlier hierarchical stages, at least in part—from the object relations point of view, this regression will be manifest in more primitive modes of interpersonal relating and experience; (5) the existence of transference in the interpersonal situation and, particularly, in the therapeutic situation—this transference will be a manifestation of the organization of intrapsychic object relations; (6) the existence of countertransference and the importance of understanding its meaning—from an object relations perspective, the countertransference may be understood as a clue to understanding what internal object relations setup is being replicated in the immediate clinical situation; (7) the value of free association, or saying freely whatever comes to the person's conscious awareness in the course of the treatment hour—articulating what is going on in the immediate interpersonal process is especially important from an object relations point of view; (8) the importance of a neutral stance on the part of the therapist, which allows the patient's self-discovery and ultimate self-determination—this neutrality will be defined for each patient in relational terms, as discussed more fully in Chapter 7; (9) the use of interpretation as a major clinical modality—with object relations in mind, interpretation will take place alongside other interventions based on the specifics of the needs of the self vis-à-vis the object; and (10) the increasing focus on the interpersonal process in the treatment situation—this process will be determined in large part by the patient's internal structure in object relations terms.

While this book discusses the object relations approach to individual psychoanalytic therapy, other authors have elucidated an object relations approach to couples therapy (Scharff and Scharff 1991) and the application of object relations concepts to family therapy (Scharff and Scharff 1989, Slipp 1984).

While the family interpersonal matrix and system requirements imposed on individuals has an impact on what is internalized and made intrapsychic, the intrapsychic object relational setup will be manifest in the dyadic dynamics of the couple. Each partner of the dyad brings his and her own world of internal object relations into the relationship. Each member has a particular transference to the partner predicated upon that structure. Couples treatment makes clear the crossed transferences and clarifies the distortions of perception that ensue. Each can come to understand and appreciate the reality of the other.

# CHAPTER 2

# Object Relations Defined

Object relations refers to the nature of the inner representational world, the nature of the various self and object representations, and their dynamic and affective interplay. A "representation" is a complex cognitive schema, an enduring organization of psychic elements – including affect and impulse – we refer to as the structure of the self or the structure of the object. The word "object" refers to the mental image of the primary caretaking other that is constructed by the very young child. These mental representations develop in a manner that is described by Piaget (1936) in his description of the evolution of cognitive schemata. The unique quality of an individual's inner world of self and object derives from his or her early experience vis-à-vis the primary caretaker, usually the mother. What is at first *interpersonal* becomes structured as enduring organizations of the mind—that is, it becomes *intrapsychic*—and then what has become intrapsychic once again becomes expressed in the interpersonal situation. These internalized relationships are generally organized with a specific self-image vis-à-vis a specific object image, and each such Gestalt is characterized by associated emotions and impulses. For example, the good self is paired with the good object and the feelings between them are love, or joy, or security, or other positive affects.

The internal object relations function as a kind of template that determines one's feelings, beliefs, expectations, fears, wishes, and emotions with respect to important interpersonal relationships. It is important to keep in mind that these intrapsychic imagoes are not exact replicas of early experience but that they are constructed by the very small child with its limited cognitive abilities and primitive mental mechanisms. The inner world is thus an amalgam of actual experience and perception, and these mental representations evolve over the early years in accordance with the child's maturing cognitive capacities and actual experience. The more pathological early development, the more likely we are to see the earliest, more "primitive" organizations present in consciousness and experienced by the individual as real in everyday life. In healthy development, the more primitive organizations are subject to repression and emerge in fantasy, dream, or artistic creation, whereas the more mature organization becomes salient in here-and-now experience.

Kernberg (1976) describes this process, saying that object relations theory stresses the simultaneous buildup of the *self* (a composite structure derived from the integration of multiple self-images) and of *object representations* (or *internal objects* derived from the integration of multiple object-images into more comprehensive representations of others). The terminology of these self and object components varies from author to author, but what is important is the essentially dyadic or bipolar nature of the internalization within which each unit of self- and object-image is established in a particular affective context.

# CHAPTER 3

# The Stages of Object Relations Development

---

The patterning of the mental schema we call *self* and the mental schema referred to as the *object* takes place in predictable, hierarchical stages. We use the term object rather than mother because this particular mental schema is in part created by the child in keeping with its own limited mental capabilities and unique experience of the early caretaking environment. In a way, the child creates a metaphor for the significant other from its interpersonal experiences. This metaphor, in turn, reciprocally shapes the child's perception and expectations of the interpersonal environment, along with the child's behavior toward it.

Freud (1912b) notes that one tends to approach every new person with anticipatory ideas and that these are directed toward the analyst. This, of course, is the essence of transference. Freud comments that "this cathexis will have recourse to prototypes, will attach itself to one of the stereotype plates which are present in the subject . . ." (p. 100). These stereotype plates are, in modern parlance, the self and object representations.

There is disagreement in the analytic literature with respect to how developmental observations should be interpreted. Stern (1985) disagrees with Mahler and others (Mahler et al. 1975), particularly with respect to the earliest intrapsychic experience of the infant. I believe that much of the disagreement is because of the failure to distinguish between *process* and *structure*. For example, human babies, like all mammals, are born with a repertoire of attachment-seeking and -evoking behaviors, such as making eye contact or molding to the mother's body, or even the ability for olfactory discrimination between mother's breast pad and that of another woman. These are behaviors that evoke reciprocal attachment-seeking behaviors in the caretaker. Yet, from the infant's point of view, the setting down of *enduring* mental connections, the emergence of an attachment as a *cognitive structure* with an established image of self and other, is not immediate.

Thus, although the infant's behavior cannot be described as "autistic," nonetheless, the absence of a mentally structured other at the start of life can be interpreted as the existence of an autistic (or objectless) state (which alternates with social interaction), a state that can be clinically observed in the case of the anaclitic depression, or in the emergence of the "black hole" (Grotstein 1990) phenomenon.

Similarly, cognitive intelligence must be distinguished from sensory-motor intelligence. Although the infant can sense the difference between what is part of its own body and what is not, it does not as yet have a *mental construct* of me/not-me. We see the failure to achieve this as a fully developed mental construct in certain patients. Even the simple mechanism of projection is a letting down of that distinction. This is another issue that has created pseudo-disagreements in the theoretical literature. Lichtenberg (1975) noted the establishment of the mental constructs as the point at which "The child . . . begins to 'live' a bit less in exclusive response to the outer world; he lives a bit more in his mind" (p. 461). That is, the internal representations that are laid down play a larger role in the child's mental activity and form the basis for fantasy formation and elaboration.

This section on hierarchical stages of object relations development borrows from Mahler and colleagues and is based on the notion of intrapsychic *structure* and its developmental vicissitudes.

As the child negotiates a series of developmental processes, beginning with the process of attachment, each stage brings it to a higher level of structural organization. The schemata of self and object—the self and object representations—become increasingly complex and increasingly differentiated from each other. At the same time, disparate aspects of the organization of the self become increasingly integrated within a single self-schema, whereas a similar process takes place with disparate aspects of object representation. Gradually, a single, integrated self representation evolves, as does a single, integrated object representation. The structuring of affect—that is, its association with a specific object relational setup—takes place within the developmental process of the evolving of object relations. Other facets of mental functioning are similarly organized *within* and *integrated with* the self representation. We can see evidence of the presence or absence of such integration on the Rorschach, where the integration of a color response into a well-formed percept is contrasted with the pure color response, an indication of the failure to integrate affect within a structured self representation.

The organization that eventuates in the self representation includes the integration of affect, of impulse (aggression and sexuality), of somatic experience, and bodily self-image. It also includes the integration of those aspects of functioning that comes about as the result of maturation—the autonomous functions of the ego—such as motor development, thought, and perception. Object relations theory is especially useful inasmuch as it forms an umbrella for the integration of concepts from diverse theoretical orientations. Failures of such integration in the mind are themselves manifestations of pathological development, whether structural or conflictual.

Each of the stages of object relations development, which are defined in terms of the nature of the self and object representations, leaves its traces in the unconscious, and even in the fully evolved individual, they may be reactivated under stress and regression, or in dream, fantasy, or artistic production. When there has not been a healthy evolution, there is evidence of early levels of organization in current interpersonal relationships, in which it is played out in the here and now. This, of course, is especially relevant to psychotherapy and the transference.

Each level of psychic organization determines to a large extent the nature of the child's experience of itself and of the other, along with characteristic interactions between the two. The individual's psychic organization is not directly observable, and, for the most part, it remains beyond conscious awareness, although what derives from it is conscious. Jacobson (1964) defines identity as the conscious experience of the self representation.

In the section on assessment of character structure (Chapter 10), reference is made to an approach to clinical assessment of object relations. In this section, I will lay out the hierarchical stages as a foundation for understanding certain clinical phenomena that become manifest in the interpersonal situation, and especially in the relationship between patient and therapist.

## THE PREATTACHMENT STAGE

Mahler (1968) refers to a state of "normal autism" as existing at birth. As noted earlier, this does not imply that the child is in a chronic withdrawn state as in the case of a state of pathological autism. However, despite the immediate activation of the hard-wired attachment process, there is as yet no enduring, structured mental representation of the object. Interpersonal experiences and their patterning and resultant memory traces are yet to come. Some might argue that the innate preference for the pattern of a facial configuration over a geometrical or other nonhuman-type pattern (Fantz 1966) indicates an innate object structure from the start. However, although the *precursors* of self and object representations may be present at birth in the form of preference, readiness, and potential, the cognitive development that is necessary for the structuring of mental schemata and for the development of structure, as we use the term, has not yet occurred.

The most clearly stage-related pathology is that of early infantile autism, in which the child remains at this infantile stage and makes no move toward attachment. Along with the absence of attachment-seeking behavior, there appears to be a basic cognitive defect in these children that interferes with the organizational processes themselves. Before these inborn deficits were discovered, the mothers of such children were branded "icebox mothers," with the asssumption that the failure of attachment in these children was the direct consequence of the failure of the mother to facilitate the process. In situations in which the environment is grossly pathological, disrupting the organizing capacities of the child, there may be a retreat into secondary autism. Autistic withdrawal in response to severe stress in an adult suggests that the failures of the environment date back to the earliest months of life.

Grotstein (1990) writes of the "black hole" and "nothingness" experience of those patients who, although functioning on a high level, may be thrust back into the primitive terrors of the preattachment stage when loss of connection with the object is experienced. Clinically, we are able to discern and articulate the kinds of defenses that individual constructed as a child in order to prevent the black hole experience from occurring. These defenses often entail a kind of adaptation to the mother in order to ensure her continuing attention. For example, we may find an individual who, in chameleon fashion, establishes an illusion of sameness in the service of the denial of separateness with its imminent threat of abandonment, object loss, and primal terror.

## THE PROCESS OF ATTACHMENT

Over the earliest months of life we see the innate attachment-seeking behavior of the infant interacting with maternal behavior and response in a manner that, optimally, brings about the subsequent stage of normal symbiosis (Mahler 1968) when the child has synthesized the experience of himself or herself in such a way as to include the primary caretaker and the salient qualities of their characteristic interaction. It is here that the basis for an affectional relationship and for what Erikson (1950) calls "basic trust" is laid down. The mother's emotional availability and her capacity for empathic response are essential to this process. In contrast, when this period is characterized by overwhelming frustration, fear, and rage in the child, we would expect a "paranoid core" to result. There may also be an associated sense of hopelessness and despair associated with an anaclitic depression. These very early depressions lend themselves to a biological interpretation when no immediate cause of depression can be discovered in the life of the adult patient. The developmental origins are obscured and thus misunderstood. A developmental, object-relational understanding of such early depression enables us to formulate what is required of the treatment relationship to help such an individual. This would be the formation of an attachment that eventually will allow the patient to internalize the therapist in such a way as to fill in what was missing structurally to start with.

At the most primitive level, failure of attachment may carry with it severe deficits in the early organization of the self. The failure to develop an attachment and to achieve a satisfactory symbiosis because of environmental failures, such as institutionalization or an unstable foster-home situation, may lead to the development of characteristic disturbances, such as the inability to keep rules, lack of capacity to experience guilt, and an indiscriminate and inordinate craving for affection with no capacity to make lasting relationships (Rutter 1974). As we might expect, the development of a superego (conscience and ego ideal), which evolves from identifications with parental figures, will not take place in the absence of those very attachments on which it depends.

There may be a disruption of attachment due to separation and loss. Subsequent development depends on the availability of a satisfactory substitute attachment object. Such interruption may lead to a lifelong schizoid detachment. Repeated disruptions of the bond between mother and infant because of the chronic illness of either of them, or because of periodic maternal depression may have the same outcome.

The quality of the child's experience during the attachment process, and during subsequent separations and losses in the first 3 years of life, builds into the inner world feelings and expectations about the interpersonal world that will color all later developmental stages as well as future interpersonal relationships. A truly reparative psychotherapy will require, first and foremost, the establishment of an attachment between patient and therapist. The resistance to the establishment of a dependent transference is likely to be a major factor in work with these patients.

## STAGE OF NORMAL SYMBIOSIS

Midway between the process of attachment and the separation–individuation process (Mahler 1968) stands the primitive mental structure, the undifferentiated self-object representation. (Note: this hyphenated self-object is not the same as Kohut's selfobject concept. The first refers to the condensed images of self and other. The second refers to the functional other, that is, what is important in the interpersonal interaction between self and other.)

Because of immature cognitive abilities, these undifferentiated images of the self and object are also not yet integrated, with disparate images existing side by side. Instead they are organized on the basis of the predominant feelings that go with the interactions between the self and the primary caretaker. The good self- and object images are linked by positive feeling and mood. The bad self- and object images are linked by negative feeling and mood. Not until the cognitive development that will come toward the end of the second year of life will the disparate images be integrated into single, cohesive representations of the self and of the other. The persistence of this split into adult life leads to an inability to hold on to relationships. When the other fails to be all good because of a failure to meet the wishes or needs or demands of the self, the other then becomes all bad and is discarded or becomes the object of intense hatred. The "character disorders" are characterized by this state of affairs. This is referred to as splitting and is a manifestation of developmental failure. Splitting may be used as a defense mechanism after integration has already taken place. It is a defense against the intolerable anxiety of intense ambivalence.

Insofar as the primary caretaker has been able to lend herself to the child's unfolding, the experience vis-à-vis the other is part of the child's positive and trusting experience of the self. Herein lies the archaic unconscious basis for the experience of oneness that at times comes with a loved other, particularly in making love and orgasm. But whatever the ecstasy of that experience, it also may carry a charge of anxiety at the felt loss of separateness of the self. Defenses against intimacy may be based on such fear.

The loss of the capacity to differentiate self from other is a serious loss of reality testing and, in the extreme, is considered a psychotic symptom. This kind of loss of reality may come and go in more severe cases of the character disorder. The borderline patient will be able to recover from momentary losses of differentiation.

The bipolarity of experience—that where attention is directed inward toward the self and that where attention is directed outward toward the other—exists from the beginning of life. It starts with the infant's alternating attention to what is happening within its own body and to the interpersonal environment that it seeks to engage. All through life these conflicting pulls will be felt in one way or another, with the intensity of the conflict dependent on the security of the sense of self and the security within the interpersonal situation. The conflict may be expressed in terms of one between identity ("being myself") and intimacy ("being close to another person") (Horner 1990).

No sooner is the symbiotic structure established intrapsychically with the organization of the undifferentiated mental representation containing both self and other in interaction than the child moves toward a new process, that of separation and individuation (Mahler et al. 1975).

## HATCHING: THE BEGINNING OF SEPARATION

Mahler (1968) emphasizes the importance of the optimal symbiosis for subsequent differentiation of the self representation from the object representation.

> The more the symbiotic partner has helped the infant to become ready to "hatch" from the symbiotic orbit smoothly and gradually—that is, without undue strain on his own

> resources—the better equipped has the child become to separate out and to differentiate his self representations from the hitherto fused symbiotic self-plus-object representation. [p. 18]

Essentially this statement acknowledges the hierarchical aspect of the developmental process. Although there may be conceptual reorganization with later developmental phases, such as adolescence, early developmental failures or deficits will make themselves known in disordered relationships and symptom development.

During the process of hatching, the mother functions as a frame of reference, a point of orientation for the individuating child. If this security is lacking, there will be a disturbance in the primitive "self-feeling," which would derive or originate from a pleasurable and safe state of symbiosis, from which the child did not have to hatch prematurely and abruptly. That is, while the self representation remains cognitively intertwined with the object representation, the loss of the object and the sense of connection with that person will evoke a sense of disorganization and dissolution of the self of which the object and the sense of connection are still a part. When the underlying psychic structure is dominated by this situation, the person may experience severe separation panics. These separations can be due to the break in the emotional connection with the significant other just as much as to an actual physical separation. It is the sense of inner connectedness that remains critical and that is so insecure. This issue will be especially relevant to the treatment situation and the therapeutic relationship. A failure of the therapeutic alliance, as due to a failure of empathy or to the therapist's vacation, may evoke these kinds of severe separation reactions.

## THE PRACTICING PERIOD: SECOND STEP IN SEPARATION AND INDIVIDUATION

From about 10 months until approximately 16 months of age, the child's focus shifts increasingly to those functions that develop as a consequence of the maturation of the central nervous system, such as locomotion, perception, language and speech development, and the learning process. These are referred to as the autonomous functions of the ego. The child is also increasingly confronted with the experience and conscious awareness of its separateness from mother as distinct psychological entities. Her ready availability when the child needs her, and the pleasure he or she derives from the mastery of new abilities, makes these small separations tolerable for the child. With the culmination of the practicing period around the middle of the second year, the toddler appears to be in an elated mood. This accompanies the experience of standing upright and walking alone. The child squeals with delight. This peak point of the child's belief in its own magic omnipotence, Mahler (1968) tells us, "is still to a considerable degree derived *from his sense of sharing in his mother's magic powers*" (p. 20).

At this point in development, the inner representation of self and other are still in great part undifferentiated, and it is the *anlage* of a pathological structure that is referred to as the "grandiose self" (Kohut 1971). It draws on the earlier experience of magical omnipotence. If things go wrong in the child's subsequent relationships with its caretakers, at a time when the child has come to realize how relatively small and dependent he or she really is, the grandiose self, now an *illusion* of omnipotence and perfection, is a defensive fall-back position. The adult who the child becomes can deny anxiety and dependency wishes as long as this inflated omnipotent self is in charge. The other is no longer of any emotional consequence. Of course, the person must go to great lengths to protect the illusion, and if it is threatened, as by poor grades in school or the loss of a job, the reaction will be severe, with the development of symptoms such as depression or suicidal behavior. Sometimes others must be debased or demeaned to protect this state of being. When this scenario is activated in the therapeutic relationship, it can be a very difficult time for the therapist, and its management is critical to the reestablishment of a positive working relationship.

Echoes of the practicing period and its magic omnipotence in the unconscious sometimes lead to persisting beliefs about the magical nature of one's abilities. Learning to walk and talk do indeed come about as if by magic, unlike the conscious effort one must make to learn the vocabulary of a foreign language at school. I have worked with some individuals who were clearly of superior intelligence and to whom early learning was effortless throughout the grade school years. Paradoxically, they were far less secure about their abilities than people of lesser innate ability. They did not connect their abilities with that sense of conscious effort that gives one a feeling of some control over what one can and cannot do. What comes by magic can also disappear by magic—one cannot rely on it.

## THE RAPPROCHEMENT PHASE AND THE RAPPROCHEMENT CRISIS

At around the age of 18 months, the toddler becomes increasingly aware of his or her separateness from mother and mother's separateness from him or her. The child's experiences with reality have counteracted any overestimation of omnipotence, self-esteem has been deflated, and the child is now vulnerable to shame. Furthermore, through dependence on the object, who is now perceived as powerful, the child is confronted with the relative helplessness of the self. There is an upsurge of separation anxiety and depressed mood. If the other uses power in a benign and helpful manner, that power is the basis for the child's sense of security. The parent who is perceived as so powerful is essentially idealized, and this kind of idealization may become manifest in adult-dependent relationships in general and in the therapy relationship in particular (the idealizing transference: Kohut 1971). If, on the other hand, parental power is experienced as against the self, as something that is not only given but also withheld, the child learns to both hate and envy the power, will develop techniques to control it, and will have fantasies of overthrowing it. Behind such controlling behavior lie insecurity and anxiety. This scenario, too, will find expression in the relationship with the therapist.

The major concern of the person who struggles with issues associated primarily with this stage of development is the loss of the support, love, and approval of the other that is feared to result from the assertion of one's own wishes or feelings and will. Still vulnerable to feelings of helplessness and shame, the person tends to idealize the other and to see that person as having the power to protect the self from these painful feelings. The other may be a parent, a spouse, or a friend. This persisting dependent way of seeing the self and the other and the expectations and demands that go with it put a strain on interpersonal relationships. These demands may be expressed as entitlements, as claims made upon the other. Although the other may be idealized, he or she is also envied and feared and is blamed when things don't go well.

The rapprochement crisis is the developmental switch-point that marks the shift from a sense of omnipotence to a sense of helplessness – from a sense of perfection to a sense of shame. Erikson (1950) notes this as a time when the child can either achieve a sense of healthy autonomy or a sense of shame. He relates the outcome in large part to the toilet-training period and to parental practices and attitudes during this period.

When prior development has not gone well, the conscious awareness of the reality of separateness and the loss of omnipotence may be very traumatic. If there are deficits in the structural organization of the self representation, either as the result of unfavorable circumstances and experience or as the result of some deficit in the child's organically based synthesizing capabilities, these deficits become evident at this time. The very awareness of the separateness of the self and the caretaker evokes tremendous separation anxiety. The child, and the adult he or she becomes, is unable to negotiate the developmental demands, and symptomatic behavior develops, such as anxious clinging. This is another example of the hierarchical nature of the developmental process.

The response of the environment to the child's growth has to allow for the child's strivings toward autonomy that conflict with the intensely felt dependency needs. The term *rapprochement* suggests the alternating moving away from mother and the return to her for emotional "refueling." Healthy parents do not have a need for the child either to stay dependent and helpless or to be completely self-reliant. They can shift their way of relating to the child in a phase-appropriate manner, being empathically in tune with the child's conflicting impulses and needs. Even with the best of parents, the child is likely to feel conflicting pulls, in both regressive and progressive directions. In this way, development is inherently conflictual and the conflict is not always due to parental insensitivities. Sometimes the best they can do is just to be there emotionally throughout the stormy times. This is the essence of what Winnicott (1965) refers to as the holding environment.

Echoes of the rapprochement crisis are heard in adolescence, and the setup in the unconscious left over from this early childhood phase of development will affect the manner in which the young person negotiates the later developmental tasks. Anxiety over self-assertion, or at the prospect of moving out of the parental home, may come from the activation of unconscious rapprochement factors. The sense of self and other is still being determined by the nature of the self and object representations that were in existence at that early time and are still making themselves felt.

The conflicts arising from this period will be very evident in the transference, where the patient fears the loss of the positive regard and support of the therapist as a retaliation for the patient's expression of his or her own feelings, wishes, or assertion of will.

## THE ACHIEVEMENT OF IDENTITY AND OBJECT CONSTANCY

With the development of language, the concepts of "mama" and "baby" are established at the start of the rapprochement period. This conceptual achievement has organizing and integrating effects. Unintegrated islands of disparate self representations and of disparate object representations become unified cognitively and structurally under the specific label, or symbol. There is a single self who may be good or bad, happy or angry, and a single object who may also be experienced in a number of different ways. This cognitive and structural integration sets the stage for an integrated sense of self, or identity, and an integrated view of the other. Although the child may be angry at the mother for some felt deprivation or failure of empathy, she is still the mother who is loved and valued in her own right, and not only for what she can do for the child's self. That is, she is far more than just a Kohutian selfobject even though she may function in that capacity at times. The love tempers the anger. We do not see the cold hate and rage characteristic of a more primitive organization and structural splitting. The individual has achieved the capacity for ambivalence, a developmental milestone. At this point, intrapsychic conflict (as contrasted with structural deficit) becomes more prominent.

In the earlier stage of development, before the cognitive achievement that brought the recognition that there is really just one self that may be experienced and expressed in a wide variety of ways, and one mother who may also call forth a variety of wishes and feelings, the self and object representations were split on the basis of the quality of feeling and emotion that went into the interaction. Mother was all good, idealized, adored, or she was all bad and hated. When hatred and the bad mother image were evoked, it was as though the good mother failed to exist, as though she had been destroyed. In therapy, resistance to (defenses against) the emergence of anger may be based on the fear of destroying the good object, the therapist.

With integration, the complex, differentiated self and the sense of having a single identity come into being and provide a foundation for an unfolding individuality. In healthy development, with a more realistic picture of the other, relationships are increasingly defined on the basis of the here-and-now interaction, although certain wishes, attitudes, and expectations, as well as the quality of emotions, are still colored by the forgotten past. Nevertheless, the degree of transference that is operating is minimal. (Transference takes place in and out of therapy.)

Although archaic self and object representations persist in the unconscious, their impact is mitigated by the ascendency of reality-dominated perception and thought. The unconscious images may appear in dreams or in fantasy or may be recreated in artistic productions. The fairy godmother and the wicked witch of the fairy tales of childhood strike a familiar chord in children and adults alike, resonating with the now unconscious split images that dominate the earliest months of life. A spate of horror movies suggests an even more frightening unconscious world that perhaps is activated by the increase in violence in the world-at-large. At times, we may yearn for the blissful oneness of symbiosis or chafe under what feels like engulfment in a relationship. But, by and large, our reality perceptions keep us firmly rooted in our own individuality and that of the other.

With the final stages of differentiation of self from object, certain identifications with the object remain as part of the self and are experienced as part of the self. The baby needed mother to comfort it and relieve its anxiety. Now the capacity to comfort the self and to relieve one's own anxiety with a variety of psychological mechanisms is part of the self, derived from what once came from outside. This transformation can be observed in process in the toddler's relationship with his teddy bear or Linus blanket—the so-called "transitional object" (Winnicott 1951).

The parents' "Good for you!" which reflected their

pleasure in the child's accomplishment, now is voiced by the part of the self referred to as the "superego" (Freud 1923a). Schafer (1960) deems this voice the "loving superego." The superego is comprised of both the ego-ideal (the self one wants to be) and the conscience. Not only does the superego criticize the self for transgressions; it also praises when one lives up to one's ego-ideal and is the source of a healthy and secure self-esteem. These identifications allow the person to do for the self what once could be done only by parental figures; they are necessary to the development of full emotional autonomy. While the "constant object" is the reliable other who provides the holding environment and whose image does not fluctuate, object constancy refers to the internalizations and identifications that result in an internal good mother, now experienced as part of the self.

## THE OEDIPUS COMPLEX AND THE EMERGENCE OF THE TRIANGLE

With the full differentiation of self from object, there is also a firmer differentiation of mother from father. The baby certainly can tell the difference between them in the early months of life, but at this higher level they become increasingly real people rather than selfobjects in the Kohutian sense. Gender becomes increasingly important and with it issues of sexuality and eroticism. Although we certainly see the pattern of the "preferred parent" emerging clearly very early—sometimes the mother and sometimes the father—the pattern of parental relationships is more one of parallel dyads. It is not until the oedipal period that the sense of triangle, of wanting and needing both and of wanting to be special to both, and the consequences of choice become salient for the child. The individuality of each parent is recognized and valued differentially. What was a dyadic view of the interpersonal world now includes *two* significant others. A two-way competitiveness within the triangle generates new wishes, anxieties, and defenses. The child wants to be preferred by mother over father and by father over mother. Along with envy, the child now experiences jealousy of a rival who is also loved. Thus, an uncomfortable ambivalence is generated. This is different from the jealousy of the new baby who is *not* also loved. In fact, the child might be very happy to dispense with it entirely.

The relative ease or difficulty of this period will be strongly influenced by prior development and by the nature of the inner representational world. The oedipal period tends to overlap with the latter part of the rapprochement phase of the separation–individuation process, so that rapprochement anxieties are aggravated by oedipal strivings. Will the little girl's move toward father be punished by the loss of maternal love? If the mother cannot support the child's emotional move toward father, there will be a failure to achieve object constancy (the maternal love that supports individuation) with a predisposition to depression when the person moves toward wished-for objects or goals. The child's ability to negotiate this troublesome period will also be affected by parental attitudes toward the child, who now presents the parents with an increasingly complex little person. When there is structural fragility as a result of early developmental trauma or deficit, the emergence of sexuality and oedipal strivings may actually traumatize the child, leading to regressive defenses and reorganization at a more primitive level. Anything that threatens the bond with the primary object in these children cannot be tolerated.

## GENDER IDENTITY

Gender identity development arises within the context of early object relations development. The basic character structure, in terms of the inner world of self and object and their dynamic interrelationship, and the integration of instinctual drive (sex and aggression) within the self representation, is laid down in the earliest years. Later development may be shaped or limited by the underlying structure, and the idiosyncratic picture that ultimately emerges for each individual will be the outcome of complex forces. Nevertheless, the core identity, the sense of self, is laid down before the secondary elaboration of the postindividuation stages of development. For this reason, the tasks of male development are far more formidable than those of the female child. And it is for this reason that nearly all gender identity disorders occur in males.

Kirkpatrick (1990) writes:

> The deep, profound, and durable female core gender identity takes its immutability . . . from psychological interaction during the first 18 months of life. . . . Boys' identity . . . like their morphology, may begin with feminine identity that is then driven by biological force, in addition to the psychological consequences of parental assignment, into a different masculine identity. The boy's masculine identity requires the intensity of male sexual drive and is confirmed by the penis, its sensation, its multiple functions, and erectile behavior. It is a secondary phenomenon and thus more fragile than the girl's gender identity. [p. 559]

The subsequent course of the core feminine identity of the girl, despite affective and attitudinal positions that develop in relation to it, will be relatively uninterrupted once established. The core feminine identity originates in the early object relations matrix, whereas the boy's gender identity relies on his ability to differentiate out of that matrix. Biological and interpersonal pressures may be in harmony with this differentiation. They may also be in conflict.

Coates (1990) found in her research of disordered gender identity in boys that extreme boyhood femininity is part of a pervasive disorder and that most of these children also met the criteria for nongender psychopathology. She reports that maternal psychopathology led to an impairment in the child's negotiation of the separation–individuation process and to the extinction of physical autonomous movement. In some cases, it may be that the effeminate boy identifies with the mother as a way to regain the lost object, perhaps in the context of intensely ambivalent or need-dominated mothering. Actually, this would be a reidentification that reinforces, rather than counteracts, the primary identification with the primary attachment object. Coates describes her model as interactionist, noting that biological, psychological, familial, and cultural influences all interact to produce the syndrome.

Greenson (1968) writes of the importance for the little boy of disidentifying from mother in the service of securing his male gender identity. Greenson uses the term *disidentify* in his discussion of the little boy's struggle to free himself from the early symbiotic fusion with mother. At the same time, he has to *counteridentify* with the father. The outcome of this process is determined by the mother's willingness to let the boy identify with the father figure, the father's availability, and the motives the father offers the child for identifying with him. Part of the motivation to identify with the father also arises out of mother's love and respect for the father. This process is compromised when the real qualities of the father make him an unacceptable model for the boy. In some instances of loss of the father through death or separation before the resolution of the Oedipus complex, the question of maleness is likely to be an issue when there are no other male figures to take his place.

> A 35-year-old homosexual man had been working through issues of separation and individuation in his psychoanalytic psychotherapy. He reported the increasing sense of masculinity that accompanied significant behavioral changes at work and in his relationships. Along with these changes he reported three disturbing dreams. In the first he dreamed he was in the town he grew up in and that the entire city was being destroyed by fire. Then he dreamed that his mother was dying of cancer, and that he was at a business meeting naked. In the final dream, he dreamed that he had slit his testicles open and removed one of his "balls." From his associations, the core relational conflict and the solution he had come to in response to that conflict were elucidated. To separate from his early attachment figures, especially his mother, was tantamount to destroying them, leaving him feeling alone and vulnerable. He added, "I'll be destroyed for destroying them." The self-castration, the compromising of his sense of maleness, the retreat from separating and individuating from mother, was the self-destructive defense he had played out for most of his life. The analytic work with his female therapist enabled these important changes in his sense of self and in his relationships.

It is critical that the female therapist be acquainted with the specifics of male gender identity development. Her attitude toward her patient's maleness and her support of it are necessary to counteract the impact of the mother who was hostile to men and to the maleness of her young son.

This is no place for the female therapist to act out any "sexual politics" issues.

Greenson (1968) poses the question of what will happen to the original primary identification with the mother of symbiosis. He also wonders how much of the boy's identification with the father is in the service of counteracting the original one with mother. He postulates that it is in this area that we may find an answer as to why so many men are uncertain about their maleness.

The little girl's wish to be like Daddy may not represent an actual identification inasmuch as it does not result in a change in the structure of the self or the superego. It may be a pseudo-identification and may represent an illusion of twinship in the service of the wish to be special to the father, especially if the daughter perceives his pleasure in her being like him or in being more like a son than a daughter. This can produce the paradoxical situation in which the daughter tries to earn oedipal specialness by being the son. This dynamic may then lead her into the situation in which she finds herself a competitor with him (and with other men later on), a situation that evokes confusion and anxiety.

A devaluation of mother and a hyper-valuation of father for a variety of reasons may lead to a *denial* of being like mother in any way and an assertion of likeness with father. These may be pseudo-identifications that play a defensive role in a conflict situation and do not necessarily lead to an actual change in the self. Schechter (1968) defines the process of identification as "the means by which part of the psychic structure of one person tends to become like that of another to whom he is emotionally related in a significant way" (p. 50). He distinguishes the *conscious wish* to become like another person, as happens in the formation of one's ideals, from the *actual* tendency to become like another, from the basic developmental processes leading to structural likeness. Defensive identification, on the other hand, does not lead to a structural change in the self representation.

In the clinical situation, the therapist looks for the kinds of developmental issues described in this chapter as they appear in the patient's material or in the therapy relationship itself. They will be used directly in the service of the patient's self-understanding, and of how it is to be in the world. They will also be used directly in the service of the psychological healing and growth of the patient.

The successful negotiation of these developmental tasks of these early years of life should result in a sense of "intrinsic power" (Horner 1989). Intrinsic power is defined in terms of *identity* (I am), *competency* (I can), and *intentionality* (I will). With a healthy sense of intrinsic power, the child should be well equipped to meet the challenges of the years ahead.

# CHAPTER 4

# The Role of Theory

## VALIDITY AND USEFULNESS

A theory is a set of principles or constructs that have explanatory value. Theories of personality are extremely complex insofar as they must account for a wide array of variables: genetic-constitutional, biochemical, environmental, and sociological. More and more there is a call for a biopsychosocial model of personality. Theories differ with respect to how much they may be based on empirical data and to what degree they rely on constructs to link and account for the data. A theory's validity and usefulness is measured by its internal consistency, by its ability to account for *all* the data, and, in the harder sciences, the ability to predict future outcomes on the basis of the hypotheses contained in the theory. Psychoanalytic theory falls short of the last of these measures because of the complexity of the variables involved, many of which may as yet be unknown or unmeasureable. However, in a broad general way we can predict how certain inadequacies of the early caretaking environment may compromise psychological development.

Psychoanalytic theory is largely derived from clinical data as well as from observations of the developing child. Thus, it is derived from both the normative and the pathological. As such, it attempts to understand both the origins and treatment of psychopathology.

The one construct that, from its inception, has distinguished psychoanalytic theory from other theories, such as learning or trait theories, is that of the unconscious. It is a construct common to all the various schools of psychoanalytic thinking. Since what we call the unconscious cannot be directly perceived, it must be considered a theoretical construct. Adler (1980), referring to the "electron" in nuclear physics and to the "black hole" in astronomy, notes that modern science legitimately and validly deals with objects that lie outside the range of ordinary experience because they cannot be directly perceived. He includes the unconscious as another example of such a legitimate and valid object of study (p. 67). He reminds us of Ockham's assertion that "we are justified in positing or asserting the real existence of unobserved or unobservable entities if—and *only* if—their real existence is indispensable for the explanation of observed phenomena" (p. 98).

Strachey (1957) wrote that the basis of Freud's repression theory of hysteria and the cathartic approach to treatment "cried out for a psychological explanation," noting that it was "only by the most contorted efforts that they had been accounted for neurologically" (p. 164). The neurological explanation disappeared in Freud's *The Interpretation of Dreams* (1900), and what Freud had written previously about the nervous system was now translated into mental terms. Strachey says that "the unconscious was established once and for all" (p. 164).

The major distinguishing factor of the various psychoanalytic theories is the basis for organizing the data to be explained. That is, each has its own "organizing principle." This understanding is a critical antidote to a tendency in psychoanalytic schools to view their own perspective as the "truth." We have to keep in mind the distinction between explanatory usefulness – which may vary from one clinical situation to another – and "truth."

Ghent (1989) reminds us that "in our field where hard facts are hard to come by, beliefs are often transacted as if they were facts" (p. 169). He writes of analytic theory that it is "ultimately a *belief* system that the analyst lives and works by (and there is no assurance that the analyst has full conscious access to the system under which he or she is really operating) . . ." (p. 170). He further points out that this belief system makes a difference in how one hears, what one hears, how one assembles what is heard, and how one conducts oneself in the treatment setting.

Maturana and Varela (1987), in *The Tree of Knowledge,* using the metaphor of the eye's blind spot, the area of the retina where the optic nerve emerges, tell us that we do not see that we do not see. They emphasize the importance of knowing about knowing, adding that there is no independent, absolute perception, that everything that is said is said by someone. These authors also remind us that the knowledge of knowledge compels us to recognize that certainty is not proof of truth. Greenson (1969) says that if he tries to imagine an analytic session with a "true believer" analyst repeating the catechism of his school, he would find it "hard to see this as a living creative experience for either the patient or the therapist" (p. 354).

Our preferred theoretical orientation, if we have one, will most probably be, to some degree, in harmony with our own psychological makeup. If it were not, it wouldn't have the ring of truth for us. Thus, we delude ourselves if we believe that our theoretical orientation is based on some entirely external standard of truth. The closer the unconscious relation between our own makeup and our theory, the more vigorously will it have to be defended in an ex-cathedra manner. The very understanding of that connection, an understanding that comes from our own therapy or analysis, will enable us to avoid forcing our patient into our own procrustean bed. Freud (1917) tells us that the shadow of the object falls upon the ego, how identification with the lost object takes the place of object love. The shadow of how we came to be is indelibly etched upon who we are. The shadow of who we are will be just as indelibly written on our work—on our choice of theory as well as on the style with which we bring this theory to bear on our clinical work.

Diagnosis is, in effect, a theory about the personality of the individual patient, and as with any good theory, there should be internal consistency and a correspondence with the observed fact. Furthermore, as new data come in, as in theory construction in general, the diagnosis may have to be modified. From our theory about the individual we also make certain predictions about what will help that individual. Perhaps it is in the clinical setting that we can best test the predictive value of our theory.

## ORGANIZING PRINCIPLES

The kinds of patterns (arrangements of data) we are likely to perceive as we build our diagnostic theory will vary according to our "organizing principle." We may come to the task with a preexisting principle in mind, or one may leap up at us from the data. By organizing principle we refer to the way we order and organize the data, the perspective from which we view those observations. A pile of wooden blocks of various colors, shapes, and sizes may be sorted according to color, according to shape, or according to size. Each sorting has a different organizing principle, and the resulting piles may look quite different from one another depending on which organizing principle was used. Beginning with the same pile of blocks, each sorting has its own inherent "truth."

Different theories of human development often start with the same "pile of blocks," with the same observations of human behavior. However, in each theory, the data are organized according to different principles. One may be no more "true" than the other. The deciding factor may be the salience of any given feature or the immediate usefulness of any given sorting. We may think in terms of psychosexual stages, in terms of Mahlerian stages of separation and individuation, or in terms of Eriksonian stages of the individual in relation to society. We may think in terms of a Freudian oedipal struggle, a Kohutian reaction to failure of empathy, a Winnicottian false-self adaptation to impingement, or even in terms of Skinnerian shaping. The "self" has become an important organizing principle for many clinicians and theoreticians.

Even Kernberg (1987) is not a strict Kernbergian. He writes:

> The Kleinian tendency to relate primitive defensive operations and object relations to the first year of life . . . or Kohut's assumption that an ever-present fragility of the self is the primary determinant . . . , or, for that matter, to consistently search for the oedipal determinants or for pathology of separation-individuation, etc., brings about an unwarranted narrowing of the interpretive frame and limits the analyst's capacity for discovering and investigating the unknown. [pp. 202–203]

If we chauvinistically cling to our own favorite organizing principle, we are likely to come to a narrowness of conclusion not unlike the conclusions of the blind men about the elephant. No matter which one we select, some other "truth" will remain unarticulated. In his editorial in *The Journal of the American Psychoanalytic Association,* Shapiro (1989) expresses his concern about the attempt of modern psychiatrists to try to use what they learn about the biological substrate of the mind in biochemical terms to explain all behavior and mood from this perspective. He notes the potential zealotry of the biologization of everything from cigar smoking to love. Shapiro adds whimsically that we cannot yet biologically distinguish hatred of one's parents from an intense dislike of broccoli. From a narrow biological bias, the elephant is neither a rope nor a tree; it is a neurotransmitter.

Noting the importance of freeing ourselves from our

theoretical belief system and referring to current controversies over the relative significance of intrapsychic conflict as contrasted with developmental defect, Ghent (1989) expresses an integrative attitude when he notes that "there will be an interaction between motivational structures that derive primarily from environmental failure with other motivational systems that collide (i.e., are in conflict) with one another" (p. 197).

There may be situations in which a particular theoretical orientation is actually *contraindicated.* I believe this is the case when one is working with an individual who was seriously abused in childhood, be it physically, sexually, or psychologically.

In my experience with such individuals who had been subjected to relentless Kleinian interpretation of what were, in effect, memories and the logical terrors associated with those memories (e.g., interpretations of them as a manifestation of infantile fantasy, of primitive greed, or as envy of the breast), it was not only a horrendous failure of empathy but also re-created the experience of abuse to such a degree that there was an iatrogenic level of terror that had become condensed with the original terror. The patients' protests may be interpreted as their envy of the breast that is trying to give them good milk and of their wish to bite it. To the patient this means that she should realize that father's penetrating her anally is for her own good, that *he* is good, and that she is bad or crazy for protesting. Indeed, the individuals I have seen who fitted this paradigm felt and, at first seemed, far "crazier" than they actually were. The fact that they also realized that their analysts were good people and really *did* want the best for them, made their "badness" all the worse. These people were not paranoid. The perceptual dissonance contributed to the near impossibility of their leaving the treatment that was making them worse in every way.

This is an example of how the treatment may be driven by the therapist's doctrinaire theoretical stance, rather than by an understanding of the person.

When we allow for multiple organizing principles, we can begin to appreciate the complexity of factors that go into the making of the mind. Inevitably, we come to a biopsychosocial model that itself is multifaceted with interactional effects thrown into the equation. If nothing else, this wider perspective should induce a proper degree of humility in any theory builder. Theory building is also the daily task of practitioner and patient as they come to an understanding of the patient's mind in terms of a number of different organizing principles. These will include constitutional givens—temperamental factors and the "fit" between the infant and its primary caretaker(s); the development of the autonomous functions that build upon the maturation of the biological organism; cognitive development as explored by Piaget, which so profoundly affects what the child does with what it experiences in its inner bodily milieu, what it experiences interpersonally, and what it experiences as it comes into contact with the nonhuman physical world and principles of time, space, and gravity. Also to be organized is the family system and its communication styles and role requirements. What a monumental task for a very small child whose cognitive capacities are so limited in a Piagetian sense!

The elaboration and emendation of the patient's theories about who he or she is, about what relationships are like, and his or her belief system with respect to acquiring and maintaining security and self-esteem regulation, leading to a resynthesis of those theories that were formulated in childhood, should be intrinsic to the therapeutic process.

Etchegoyen (1982) describes this process as follows:

> The psychoanalytic method shows the historical truth (psychic reality), not the material truth which is unattainable in its infinite variety. Each of us keeps a set of memories and beliefs that, processed into a series of *theories,* regulate our relationship with the world. The purpose of analysis is not to correct facts from the past but to *reconceptualize* them. The aim of the analytical process is to review the patient's theories and make them more rigorous and flexible. [p. 73]

The historical buildup of psychoanalytic theory and its continuing elaboration by numerous contributors to the psychoanalytic literature provides a rich tapestry of understanding and a powerful tool for our clinical work. The fragmentation of psychoanalysis, theoretically and politically, robs us of that richness and threatens the integrity of our work. Although the organizing principle emphasized in this book is object relations, it does not advocate a theoretical rigidity that might create blind spots in the clinical situation. An attitude of creative synthesis is suggested when clinically appropriate and useful.

# CHAPTER 5

# The Goals of Treatment

Just as in the formulation of a diagnosis (which is a theory about how a particular individual is put together psychologically), the formulation of the goals of treatment must be specifically tailored to and appropriate for any given patient. We may draw up broad general guidelines concerning "what cures," but, as we see in the literature, the notion of what cures is usually consistent with the author's theoretical point of view.

## RESOLUTION OF CONFLICT

Freud (1933a, p. 80), writing from the perspective of his structural theory in which he formulated the concepts of id, ego, and superego, put forth as the goal of psychoanalysis, "Where id was, there ego shall be." As he put it elsewhere (1923*b*), "Psycho-analysis is an instrument to enable the ego to achieve a progressive conquest of the id" (p. 56).

When the diagnosis is one of neurotic conflict, anxiety, and defense—as in the case of the Oedipus complex—analysis of anxiety and defense and resolution of the underlying unconscious conflict will be viewed as the path to cure.

## MODIFICATION OF PATHOLOGICAL STRUCTURES

If a character diagnosis reveals the existence of a false self (Winnicott 1965), which is an adaptation that was developed in the early years as a way to protect the true self from the dangers of an abandoning/impinging interpersonal environment while at the same time finding a way to stay connected to the needed other, the view of what cures and the goal of treatment will be consistent with that formulation. By providing a safe "holding environment," therapist and patient together will find the hidden, split-off true self, bring it into relationship with the therapist, and enable the individual to integrate it with those development achievements that were experienced through the false self. The individual will then be able to take up an authentic life lived primarily through the true self.

Another example of modification of pathological structure as a treatment goal is the healing (integration) of the split between affectively positive (good) self and object representations and affectively negative (bad) self and object representations. The interpersonal therapeutic matrix is the medium within which this integration takes place. What is achieved is the capacity for ambivalence toward the self and toward important others.

Integration of split-off affect within a cohesive self, and the establishment of psychological boundaries between the self and others are further examples in which the emphasis is on the importance of modifying pathological structure.

Horowitz (1990) describes how the schemas of the self and the other change through the phases of the mourning process, and he notes that the work of schematic change is slow. He notes that the schematic changes that go with completion of the mourning process are like similar changes that take place through resolution of the transference or through the developmental course of identification. Schemas, the inner representations of the self and the object, cannot be quickly altered. Such alteration is the goal of a treatment aimed at modifying pathological structure as well.

Segal (1982) succinctly summarizes the relationship between pathological structure and how it is modified in psychoanalytic treatment.

> Patients come to us with their internal world structured in a particular way. As the transference develops they project their internal objects and parts of themselves on to us in a way which reveals the object relationships, anxieties and defenses underlying the structure of their personality; the situation becomes dynamic again, and we discover the early infantile conflicts and object relationships which led to the creation of those particular structures. Transference is not a simple repetition of childhood . . . the psychoanalytical process modifies the nature of internal figures and relation-

> ships. Thus, in analysis we are dealing not only with the historical past but also, dynamically, mostly with an ahistorical past which keeps changing and altering in the psychoanalytic process. Such historical past . . . is relived . . . in terms of evolving internal dynamics of the transference relationship. [p. 15]

Through the treatment process, the primitive experience "can be integrated, symbolized and partly at least verbalized" (p. 21).

Kernberg and colleagues (1989) describe the process specifically in reference to the borderline patient.

> Expressive psychotherapy for borderline psychopathology is designed to enhance the borderline patient's ability to experience self and others as coherent, integrated, realistically perceived individuals, and to reduce the need to use defenses that weaken ego structure by reducing the repertoire of available responses. As a result, the patient may be expected to develop an increased capacity to control impulses, tolerate anxiety, modulate affect, sublimate instinctual needs, develop stable and satisfying interpersonal relationships, and experience intimacy and love. [p. 8]

The structural underpinnings of the internal self and object world are addressed in terms of boundary structuring, an integration and thus cohesion of various aspects of self and object, and an integration of split representations that paves the way to the capacity to perceive others realistically. These structural changes enable the further changes of behavior described by these authors.

## REPAIR OF STRUCTURAL DEFICIT

Kohut (1984) views psychopathology in terms of damage to the self that was the result of disturbances in the person's early self–selfobject relationships, that is, in the relationship with the primary caretaker in the earliest years and beyond. This does not sound very different from other theories about the effects of disturbed early, primary relationships. What is different is how the role of the caretaker is conceptualized by Kohut in terms of her function and her responsibility to empathically mirror the child to itself in a way that enhances the development of a cohesive and positively regarded self. It is that function that defines the selfobject. Sometimes the concept is misinterpreted as necessarily a positive reflection of the self. An empathic response makes the individual feel seen and heard, enhancing his or her sense of existing and cohesion and counteracting the often-felt sense of self-annihilation of individuals with structural deficit.

Empathy as a concept is not the invention of or possession of self psychology. As Levy (1985) notes:

> Empathy in its popular usage refers to the capacity of one person to communicatively partake, in a limited way, in the experience of another. . . . Empathy as a term has its place as descriptive of the analyst's emotional relatedness to the patient. It does not refer to any specific psychoanalytic technical intervention or theoretical construct; rather, it describes in a general way the sensitive, tactful, and experience-near way in which the analyst approaches the inner life of his patients. [p. 376]

Empathy should be the tool of every therapist, regardless of his or her theoretical orientation. It is a combination of listening to and being with the patient.

Kohut's (1984) concept of cure is consistent with his theory of normal and pathological development insofar as cure, from his perspective, lies in the transformation of the self–selfobject relationships. He writes, "Self psychology holds that self–selfobject relationships form the essence of psychological life from birth to death" (p. 47). The self–selfobject relationship is one in which the significant other is experienced as necessary to the sense of self-cohesion and worth. It is, in the view of self psychologists, a dependent aspect of being that is not outgrown, that is lifelong, and that goes two ways in relationships, which are always interdependent.

When an individual's earliest caretakers failed to enhance the development of cohesion and worth, the person will continue to look to others to serve that function, usually in immature ways that do not work in adult life. What cures, from Kohut's frame of reference, is "the opening of a path of empathy between self and selfobjects, that is, the establishment of empathic intuneness between self and selfobjects on mature adult levels" (p. 66). Enabling this process is the self psychologist's goal of treatment. This goal is reached through the analysis of defenses within the context of the therapeutic relationship and through the unfolding of the transference. These two elements are common to other theoretical orientations as well, although the nature of the specific interpretations and how the transference is viewed and referred to will differ in other theoretical contexts. From the self psychology perspective, when empathic intunedness is established, the individual is safe to resume healthy development in a way that provides new structures that will fill in defects and firm up the cohesion of the underlying structure of the self, and that will enable the person to establish what self psychologists view as mature self–selfobject relationships. The *specific* and *idiosyncratic* nature of the structured internal world, how it developed and how it is now replicated in the interpersonal situation, is not specifically addressed. The interpersonal process is looked at in terms of the self and the selfobject *function* of the other.

To return to the previous chapter and the role of theory, if one adheres in a doctrinaire manner to a specific theoretical orientation, one will also have a narrower vision of what cures and thus a narrower range of clinical choices. The more the therapist is able to integrate conceptually the "truths" of the various psychoanalytic perspectives, the greater the potential precision of understanding how the patient is organized psychologically, and the greater the potential precision with respect to understanding and implementing what is needed by a given individual in order to move beyond the developmental impasses that originated in specific phases of early life. This should enable the individual to lead a more fulfilling life.

Somewhere, apart from its trunk, its tail, or its legs, there is an elephant, with its own intrinsic elephantness. An openness to a broader explanatory armamentarium will help the therapist apprehend the unique personhood of the patient who sits across from him or her in the consultation room, and in so doing offer the individual a relationship in which that unique personhood has the opportunity to evolve in ways that enhance the patient's sense of well-being and opportunity in the world.

## THE HEALING FUNCTION OF THE THERAPEUTIC PROCESS: THE THERAPIST AS A CONTAINING COMPANION IN THE SEARCH THROUGH MEMORY

One of the most important functions of the infant's caretakers is to step in to soothe or comfort when necessary so that the child's distress does not reach an overwhelming level. By overwhelming, we mean that the child's sense of self and self-organization is disorganized by affect that has reached traumatic proportions (Krystal 1978). Children who are subjected to chronic traumatic affect (Khan 1963) develop rigid characterological defenses against affect and its disorganizing potential.

For some patients who had to endure situations or events that were accompanied and followed by secret and lonely anguish during their developing years, a distinguishing factor was the intense sense of aloneness and inability to reach out for help. They had to figure out what was going on both within themselves as well as around them with only the resources of a young child. They had to contain their own fear, grief, rage, guilt, or shame with no kind intercessions to keep these feelings from escalating to overwhelming proportions. They developed a variety of character defenses, such as emotional detachment or obsessive-compulsive rituals, that may have been sexual in nature, or identity-disfiguring splitting off and repression of important aspects of their innately endowed talents. Creativity inherently must draw from the full reservoir of the mind. Patients describe as healing the remembering or reexperiencing of early traumatic events in the comforting presence of the therapist. "Having you with me makes it not so frightening," one woman said. "It changes the experience from something intolerable to something I can live through and triumph over."

Most people can endure great travail if there is a comforting and caring presence. A man who had been rescued two weeks after being buried in the rubble of an earthquake was quoted on a newscast as saying he had tried to kill himself. Worse than anything was the terror of being alone.

The therapist provides a caring and comforting presence as the patient negotiates the painful memories that in effect return him to those times of life that were so dreadful that he did equally terrible things to himself in order to escape the original pain. This reexperiencing in the presence of the caring and empathic other leads to a transformation of character in which the identity-distorting defenses can be relinquished and important repressed facets of the personality can be reclaimed and the self can be reintegrated. I am using the term "reintegration" here in recognition of the fact that I am referring in this section to people who had cohesive and differentiated core selves, but whose development was seriously impacted by such things as parental alcoholism or family system aberrations. These are people who suffered chronic trauma within the context of the family, and, although the trauma may have appeared to be nonviolent (such as being made the butt of sibling teasing), it did inner violence to the child's spirit and sense of identity.

Guntrip (1975) wrote:

> I can hardly convey the powerful impression it made on me to find Winnicott coming right into the emptiness of my "object relations situation" in infancy with a non-relating mother. . . . Winnicott had come into living relation with precisely that earlier lost part of me that fell ill because mother failed me. He had taken her place and made it possible and safe to remember her in an actual dream-reliving of her paralysing schizoid aloofness. [p. 153]

The therapist as companion in the search for memory and the reexperiencing of its affect enables the patient to redirect himself or herself along the healthier road that could not be traveled the first time around.

## DYNAMIC FORMULATIONS

Ingram (1987) looks at the desired outcome in dynamic terms. From a Horney perspective he writes:

> . . . one major accomplishment in a successful analysis is the expansion of the patient's capacity to contain pain, to postpone gratification—to suffer, yet to suffer without despair and without resorting to the host of . . . defensive maneuvers. . . . The well analyzed person . . . may experience greater degrees of suffering [in life] but more effectively tolerates it. . . . Far from being merely a consolation, this is properly viewed on the contrary as a major value of reduced alienation and growth of the real self. [unpublished paper]

# Part II

---

# Basic Concepts

This section will clarify some of the basic concepts of psychodynamic, psychoanalytic, developmental, and clinical theory. The term *clinical theory* refers to an attempt to conceptualize how certain phenomena of personality that have developmental origins become manifest and are addressed in the treatment situation.

# CHAPTER 6

# Transference and Countertransference

## PROCESS OR CONTENT?

*Content* refers to what your patients report, what they say about their current life, their past, or even their dreams. *Process* refers to the interpersonal milieu in which the reporting takes place. For example, if Mr. T. brings in his dreams dutifully every session but does not seem interested in understanding them, it may be more productive to explore the process—the fact of his bringing in his dreams dutifully—than to try to understand the content, the reported dream itself. We might conjecture that Mr. T.'s wish to please the authority figure—the therapist in this case—is what is really at issue. Perhaps a concomitant wish to thwart may be manifest in his lack of interest in the meaning of the dream. If compliance-defiance is a pattern of relating to others to whom he gives parental power, we need to understand this behavior in developmental-structural and dynamic terms in order to help Mr. T. understand this maladaptive pattern in a manner that will make him feel understood and helped rather than accused or criticized. All of this follows from attention to the interpersonal process revealed in the reporting of dreams in this example.

The transference is revealed in the interpersonal process. Very often an evoked countertransference is the only cue that a subtle playing out of a transferential scenario is taking place. That is, a reaction in the therapist is evoked by the patient's behavior and especially when the individual is using projective identification (see p. 79). The process is often subtle, almost invisible, were it not for the therapist's attention to the cues he or she attends to within himself or herself. In the above example, the therapist's building frustration and irritation at Mr. T.'s indifference to an analytic exploration of his dreams would lead him or her to consider possible process issues and to understand them from the interpersonal perspective. It may be likely that the content of Mr. T.'s dreams will be consistent with what is being played out interpersonally, but their interpretation is far more likely to be productive once the process has been articulated.

Etchegoyen (1982) notes that "transference analysis distinguishes the past from the present, discriminates between the objective and the subjective. When this is attained, the past need not be repeated and remains as a reserve of experiences which are useful to understand and predict the future, not to misunderstand them" (p. 73).

## KINDS OF TRANSFERENCE

### Reactions to the Therapist

It may be useful to think of transference as analogous to a subject's response to a Rorschach blot. Although all subjects may see (perceive through their visual sensory apparatus) the same blot, the wide range of differing responses is indicative of the extent to which people bring their own unique interpretations—i.e., meanings—to that which they perceive. The more that response is determined by idiosyncratic inner psychological forces, the less the response will be determined by the actual blot itself. This gives us some information about the individual's readiness to distort what goes on in the external world to make it conform to the private, inner world. Every therapist presents a particular "shape," unique qualities of style, as well as gender, age, and so on, to which people respond differently, according to their own history, belief system, expectations, fears, wishes, and feelings. This differential response, the *meaning* to the patient of what is perceived *about* the therapist, is transference. It may also be based on the therapist's professional role to which power and authority are attributed. The authority figure "shape" will evoke the patient's idiosyncratic reactions to such figures. Or, in cases of greater pathology, simply the therapist's existence as a separate person in the room will evoke responses determined far more by the patient's character structure than by what others might actually observe about the therapist. For example, if the person fears being taken over by the other or being engulfed by the other, just the therapist's presence may be experienced as a threat.

In any event, transference is based on meanings evoked in the patient's mind. For example, if the personal style of the therapist can be described in general as soft-spoken, one person may attribute kindness to this behavior while another may attribute weakness. These attributions are manifestations of transference. The concept can be extended to the therapist's activity, such as the making of an interpretation. Assuming the interpretation is correct, timed appropriately, and made with careful consideration of its effect on the patient, it can be experienced at one moment as helpful and at another as hostile criticism. These are simple examples of transference reactions. Needless to say, it becomes much more complex at times.

Even when there is something about the therapist's behavior that is obvious and clearly perceived by the patient, what the patient does with this behavior must be noted. This reaction may be blatant or subtle and will evoke a lesser or a greater transference distortion.

Let us suppose that the therapist did not sleep well the previous night because the new baby was up crying for most of the night. It is obvious that he is tired and he is less active than usual as a result. One patient may notice this and comment, "I can see you're tired. I guess you've had a hard day." Although he does not see the tiredness as having anything to do with himself, he has made an interpretation of why the therapist is tired and embedded in that interpretation may be an unconscious fantasy of what made it a hard day. There may be a fantasy that other patients are more difficult than he is himself and that they have worn the therapist out. This might have as its historical roots memories and feelings about how tired mother used to be because she had to take care of the new baby and was less available for the self. This association may be totally unconscious and, unless the therapist inquires further about the comment about the hard day, will remain unconscious.

Another patient might say, "I see how tired you are. I feel guilty about making you have to work." This patient may not take the tiredness personally but does take on herself the responsibility for taking care of the therapist, a response readiness that says something about her personality makeup, something that also has historical roots and associated memories, wishes, and feelings, all of which will go unexplored if the therapist does not pick up on the casual comment concerning his tiredness.

A third patient, on the other hand, may take what he perceives far more personally, and his interpretation may have negative implications. He might interpret the tiredness and lessened activity as anger and may assume that the therapist is angry at him for something he did the previous session, or just because he is who he is, or because at an unconscious level he is very angry at the therapist and has an equally unconscious fantasy that the therapist knows about this anger and is retaliating. In this example, we see how much greater the distortion is and how much more the response to the therapist's behavior is determined by idiosyncratic psychological forces within the patient.

All of these are examples of *transference reactions* to the therapist. The more subtle the embedded transference reaction, the more important it is for the therapist to wonder aloud about it. For example, the therapist might reply to the first patient's apparently casual comment about the tiredness saying, "Yes. You are perceiving me accurately. I wonder what the effect of my tiredness is on you." One patient might answer with some irritation, "I can't help but wonder if I'm getting my money's worth today." This answer reveals something about how the patient feels about having to pay for treatment and about concerns about being cheated out of what he feels entitled to. On the other hand, if the therapist picked up on the comment about the hard day, the session would take a different direction. The inquiry concerning the effect of the tiredness on the patient would have revealed more about the interpersonal process within the treatment relationship, whereas the inquiry concerning the fantasy of the hard day would be a response to content and would have revealed memories and feelings. Obviously, one cannot go in two directions at once, but when one is chosen, the therapist should keep in mind the undone work of the other direction and pursue it when the timing seems correct.

### A Characteristic Mode of Relating

Transference refers not only to the patient's *reactions* to the therapist based on meaning attributed to his or her behavior or demeanor but also to the patient's *way of relating* to the therapist when this way of relating is predominantly determined by unconscious or conscious expectations or defenses. For example, the patient may behave in a compliant and deferential manner toward the therapist out of anxiety that if he or she were not to do so, the therapist would become angry much as mother or father used to.

Still more complex are those ways of relating that are determined by the particular structural pathology of the patient. For example, the patient who has a "false self" identity based on the caretaking role developed vis-à-vis a psychologically fragile mother will relate in that same caretaking mode with the therapist, taking care not to say anything that might hurt the therapist's feelings.

These ways of relating that are part of the individual's character makeup, such as passive-dependent or passive-aggressive, are ways the individual relates to others in his or her everyday life. Needless to say, such characteristics affect relationships in negative ways. These central aspects of character, of the individual's way of being in the world, must be confronted in the treatment relationship and explored. They are defensive postures that have embedded within them conflictual feelings, wishes, and impulses and the defenses against the dangers of these feelings, wishes, or impulses. These defensive postures vis-à-vis the therapist are still transference even though they may not be specific to the therapist or to anything he or she says or does.

## Projection

The patient may project onto the therapist (1) his or her own thoughts or feelings, such as believing the therapist is angry when it is the patient who is actually angry, (2) thoughts or feelings characteristic of a parent with the expectation that the therapist is taking the same stance as the parent does now or did in the past, such as disapproval of a certain kind of behavior, or (3) a complete image of the self or of the important other (self and object representations) from the inner world of object relations, a form of projection referred to as *projective identification*.

In the third case, the therapist is related to as though he or she actually were the projected self or the projected object, or significant early caretaker, a powerful process that may actually induce in the therapist feelings or behaviors associated with the identity that has been projected into him or her. That is, a particular self representation or object representation is projected and the entire original gestalt of the self-in-interaction-with-object, which becomes structured as an internal object relation set-up, is externalized, replicated, and made real in the here and now. For example, a victimized self vis-à-vis the sadistic object interaction may be replicated with the therapist on one end or the other of the interaction.

Bion (1959) described the effect on the therapist as follows:

> Now the experience of counter-transference appears to me to have quite a distinct quality that should enable the analyst to differentiate the occasion when he is the object of a projective identification from the occasion when he is not. The analyst feels he is being manipulated so as to be playing a part, no matter how difficult to recognize, in somebody else's phantasy—or he would do it if it were not for what in recollection I can only call a temporary loss of insight, a sense of experiencing strong feelings and at the same time a belief that their existence is quite adequately justified by the objective situation without recourse to recondite explanation of their causation. [p. 149]

Bion notes further that one must be able to shake oneself out of this numbing feeling of reality in order to give a correct interpretation.

## COUNTERTRANSFERENCE

The term *countertransference* refers to the therapist's reactions to the patient that have dynamic significance either within the therapist or within the interpersonal matrix. These reactions may be to the patient as a person (young or old, male or female, attractive or unattractive), to the patient's material, or to the patient's behavior in the session and vis-à-vis the therapist.

Freud first made note of the phenomenon in 1910 when he wrote:

> We have become aware of the "counter-transference," which arises in the physician as a result of the patient's influence on his unconscious feelings, and we are almost inclined to insist that he shall recognize his counter-transference in himself and overcome it. [p. 144]

Thus, the classical position has been that the emergence of countertransference indicates need for further personal analysis by the therapist. This would still be the case when the therapist's own defenses against unresolved conflict (i.e., oedipal) results in his or her avoidance of the patient's material when it threatens those defenses. In my teaching and consulting experience, I find again and again that therapists are far more comfortable dealing with preoedipal issues or aggression than they are in dealing with sexuality. As a result, they sometimes collude with the patient's resistances to the uncovering and working through of sexual memories, feelings, or impulses, especially when they arise in the transference.

Some countertransference reactions are a simple empathic resonance with the patient's affect. A detached patient may make the therapist feel sleepy or bored. An anxious patient may evoke nonspecific anxiety in the therapist. How the therapist makes use of this affective information will depend on a clinical decision with respect to the timing and quality of the intervention. If one is struggling to stay awake, one might ask what the patient is experiencing at the moment. The response might open the door to an exploration of the need for detachment at that point in the session.

In recent years, with the growing focus on the interpersonal process and the effects that the participants have on one another, countertransference has come to have an additional informative value. It is often viewed as an indication of the therapist's empathic connection with the patient. That is, the therapist's openness to what is being communicated by the patient in a variety of ways sets the stage for the countertransference reaction.

Kernberg (1965) summed up the change in emphasis as follows:

> Two contrasting approaches in regard to the concept of countertransference could be described. Let us call the first the "classical" one, and define its concept of transference as the unconscious reaction of the psychoanalyst to the patient's transference. . . . This approach also tends to view neurotic conflicts of the analyst as the main origin of the countertransference.
>
> Let us call the second approach the "totalistic" one; here countertransference is viewed as the total emotional reaction of the psychoanalyst to the patient in the treatment situation. This school of thought believes that the analyst's conscious and unconscious reactions to the patient in the treatment situation are reactions to the patient's reality as well as to his transference, and also to the analyst's own reality needs as well as to his neurotic needs. This second approach implies that these emotional reactions of the analyst are intimately fused, and that although countertransference should certainly be resolved, it is useful in gaining more understanding of the patient. In short, this approach uses a broader definition of countertransference and advocates a more active technical use of it. [p. 38]

Racker (1968) refers to the therapist's experience of feelings similar to those of the patient as *concordant countertransference.* For example, the therapist may experience him- or herself as drowning in feelings of helplessness that match those of the patient. Such concordant identifications with the self-image that the patient has projected is a source of empathic understanding for the therapist as long as he or she is able to keep clear the boundary between his or her own self and that of the patient—that is, as long as the therapist is able to know what the patient feels through an empathic identification with him without losing the ability to work with it analytically. If the therapist is overcome by the helpless feelings as in the example above, rather than being able to make an empathic response about how frightening it is to feel so helpless and to link these feelings with earlier childhood helplessness, the therapist becomes impotent or immobilized. Tansey and Burke (1989) relate the therapist's ability to tolerate the countertransference to empathy and note that barriers to the empathic process may occur (1) in the reception phase, (2) in the therapist's internal processing phase, or (3) in the communication (interpretation) phase. They write:

> . . . the empathic process not only involves taking in the patient's influence (Reception), followed by analyzing and arriving at tentative understandings of this material (Internal Processing), but also entails the process of "giving back" to the patient. Questions of what, when, and how a therapist communicates to a patient, both with respect to verbal (especially interpretive) and nonverbal channels, are not merely matters of technique and timing. Answering these technical questions requires an immediate and in-depth empathic sensitivity to the patient and *to the status of the interaction* (emphasis added). [p. 99]

The issue of technique in psychoanalytic therapy always comes back to the unique situation of the clinical moment with a particular patient.

In the case of a *complementary countertransference* identification (Racker), the therapist becomes identified with the self vis-à-vis the object or with the object vis-à-vis the self. An entire early object relationship has been activated, with both parties being replicated in the here and now of the treatment situation. The gestalt of victim and persecutor is an example of this situation, a situation in which the therapist may feel his or her own sadistic impulses becoming mobilized. When this happens, there is a danger that the original relationship may be replicated in the treatment situation. The handling of complementary counteridentifications will often be very difficult because of the intensity and confusing sense of realness of the associated feelings and impulses that have been evoked in the therapist by the patient's behaviors. When the therapist is unable to maintain the boundary between his or her own sense of self and the complementary counteridentification, there is danger of the therapist's acting out in a way that leads to a replication of the early trauma for the patient. When there is a loss of boundaries, or when the reenactment revives the therapist's own unresolved conflict, or when the therapist's cognitive functioning is temporarily impaired by the intensity of feelings that have been evoked through the projective identification, these feelings will not be useful as an empathic source of understanding for the therapist. A clear sense of self enables the therapist to make use of his or her complementary transference feelings as a source of empathy and understanding concerning the patient's developmental traumas, which have become internalized and are part of his internal representational world. The interpretation of these recognitions by the therapist may or may not be useful at the time they occur. The patient's capacity to stand back and to observe himself at the time (the availability of an observing ego), the state of the therapeutic alliance (feelings of trust toward the therapist), and of the working alliance (the ability to do the work of therapy at the moment), will tell the therapist whether an interpretation can be tolerated at the time.

# CHAPTER 7

# Neutrality

## CLINICAL ATTITUDE

Watzlawick and colleagues (1967) remind us that we "cannot not communicate." Neutrality is not so much a prescribed behavior as it is an attitude toward the patient as well as toward the work. Poland (1984) defines neutrality as originating in "genuine respect for the patient's individuality . . . [a] fundamental regard for the essential otherness of the patient, for the uniqueness of the patient's self in its own right . . ."

(pp. 285–286). Greenberg (1986) believes that neutrality is "a way of affirming our own commitment to exploration and self knowledge in contrast to other therapeutic aims" (p. 82).

## CLINICAL RATIONALE

There is also a clinical rationale for neutrality as well as a philosophical attitude. Wachtel (1986) points out that "the stance of neutrality is designed to assure that we do not muddy the waters of transference." But he also speaks to the inevitability of our influencing the process even as we observe it. "We are always observing something in relation to us, and not just to us as screens or phantoms, but to us as specific flesh and blood human beings sitting in the consultation room" (p. 61).

Greenberg provides us with a clinically useful definition of neutrality that allows for its application in a manner specific and appropriate to the uniqueness of any given patient. He agrees with Schafer (1983) that there is an intimate connection between the analyst's neutrality and the patient's experience of safety, without which he or she would continue to feel "injured, betrayed, threatened, seduced, or otherwise interfered with or traumatized" (p. 32). Schafer tells us that "there is always room in analytic work for courtesy, cordiality, gentleness, sincere empathic participation and comment, and other personal, although not socially intimate, modes of relationship" as well as a "respectful affirmative attitude" and an attitude of "appreciation" (p. 32). Neutrality is not manifest in a "deadpan" facial expression when one goes to meet the patient in the waiting room, nor is it manifest in the failure to inquire as to the well-being of a loved one after a cancellation due to a mother's or child's surgery.

## THE THERAPEUTIC RELATIONSHIP AND NEUTRALITY

Neutrality is manifest in the therapeutic relationship and its expression is specific to the patient's psychological makeup, to the nature of his or her internal world of self and object representations, which are the basis of wishes and fears, hopes and dreads. In other words, what is or what is not neutral depends on the individual in question. What is neutral for one is abandonment for another. What is caring for one is impinging for another. Our clinical concepts cannot be truly understood abstractly but must be placed in a clinical context.

Here again Greenberg (1986) offers a clinically useful approach to understanding neutrality. "Neutrality embodies the goal of establishing an optimal tension between the patient's tendency to see the analyst as an old object [transference] and his capacity to experience him as a new one" (p. 97). The potential for change lies in new and healthier experience. Greenberg writes:

> The patient can become aware that he is assimilating the analyst into his world of archaic internal objects only when he has already become aware that there is an alternative possibility. . . . If the analyst cannot be experienced as a new object, analysis never gets under way; if he cannot be experienced as an old one, it never ends. [p. 98]

Greenberg is pointing out that if the situation is too safe and there is no room for transference to emerge, the patient will not have the opportunity to confront the threatening feelings that are part of an archaic relationship. If the therapist is also afraid of the emergence of these feelings, he or she is likely to behave in ways that are unconsciously aimed at reducing or negating the potential for transference. Neutrality implies neither forcing transference nor evading it. Greenberg notes that neutrality is measured by the patient's ability both to become aware of the transference and to tolerate it.

The concept of neutrality as a midpoint position is consistent with the classical view of it as siding neither with the id nor with the superego, neither with the wish or impulse nor with the taboo against it. Similarly, the neutral therapist does not side with either direction of the patient's ambivalencies.

# CHAPTER 8

# The Frame

Langs (1979a) defines the therapeutic frame as a "metaphor for the implicit and explicit ground rules of psychotherapy or psychoanalysis" (p. 540). He notes that these ground rules "create a distinctive set of conditions within the frame [of the treatment situation] that differentiate it in actuality and functionally from conditions outside the frame" (p. 540). However, he does emphasize that the metaphor requires "an appreciation of the human qualities of the frame and should not be used to develop an inanimate or overly rigid conception" (p. 540). Unfortunately, many therapists do indeed erect overly rigid frames that do not allow for Schafer's notion that "there is always room in analytic work for courtesy, cordiality, gentleness, sincere empathic participation and comment, and other personal, although not socially intimate, modes of relationship . . ." (p. 32). The whole issue of neutrality is directly related to the concept of the frame and can be considered an instance of it.

Greenson (1971) points out the difference between "unanalytic" procedures and "antianalytic" procedures. An antianalytic procedure is one that blocks or lessens the patient's capacity for insight and understanding. "Any measure which diminishes the ego's function or capacity for observing, thinking, remembering, and judging would fall into this category." Under these conditions the patient may develop "more doubts about his ego functions and his capacity to empathize, all of which would have impaired his capacity for sound ego functioning and retarded his analysis" (pp. 359–386). An unanalytic procedure may deviate from the standard techniques but it still furthers the course of the treatment. Greenson's views are useful in decisions with respect to what constitutes an appropriate attendance to the frame and what may constitute an overly rigid or overly flexible attitude toward it.

Langs differentiates aspects of the "fixed" frame—such as fee, time, and length of sessions, the physical setting, and total confidentiality and privacy—from the "variable" frame that allows for humanness on the part of the therapist. Sometimes frame decisions are not all that clear. Are telephone calls considered as legitimately within the frame when occasioned by disturbance that requires therapeutic intervention? That would be my view. On the other hand, what about those calls that constitute an acting out by the patient as a means to extract more time and concern from the therapist? The frame can be broken by either patient or therapist, and when the patient violates the frame, the therapist may feel less safe, a situation that will probably evoke countertransference defenses. Both parties have to feel safe enough for the work to proceed as it should. In the instance of the phone call that lies within the frame (despite its taking place outside the scheduled hour and place), one does whatever work is necessary. When the call violates the frame, the acting out needs to be interpreted in order to further the analytic work and contained in order to protect the arena of safety that must surround the work.

## LIMIT SETTING

Limit setting may be necessary to protect the frame. When the limit setting leads to feelings of endangerment in the patient rather than increased safety, this may be due to the therapist's misreading of the behavior in question, a failure to realize that the situation is not one of an acting out that needs to be contained and interpreted but as a crisis that needs attending to. Of course, acting out may itself create a crisis so that both management and interpretation will be indicated. A nonempathic attitude in the setting of limits may also lead to feelings of endangerment in the patient. Interpretation of acting out behavior is best done in a manner that indicates a wish to understand its psychological meaning rather than in a punitive way.

An example of the breaking of the frame by the patient is the situation in which the patient discusses the treatment with someone else, inviting comments, and bringing these comments back to the therapist. This kind of triangulation and its structural and dynamic implications need to be explored and understood. Understanding should lead to a cessation of the behavior. If the therapist merely interdicts the behavior, the dynamics of the triangulation become further complicated. Such interdiction would be considered antianalytic in Greenson's sense, whereas useful limit setting may be simply unanalytic.

Sometimes, although the patient may not like the limit setting, it may actually produce an increased sense of safety in knowing that his or her destructiveness will not be allowed to endanger the treatment.

Sometimes limit setting is difficult for a therapist whose philosophy is essentially antiauthoritarian and who is not comfortable taking a prohibiting stance. Attending to countertransference resistances to doing what needs to be done to protect the frame will help the therapist make appropriate clinical decisions and act upon them.

When it is the therapist who acts in a manner that endangers the frame, self-monitoring and analysis of the behavior may reveal something about the process that will lead to a further understanding of the patient. This situation frequently prevails when the patient uses projective identification.

## THE SUBSTANCE-ABUSING PATIENT

Substance abuse is a situation in which I believe it is necessary to set limits. Not only does this form of acting out stand as a massive resistance to the treatment process, but the effect of the drug itself on the personality, mood, and mental functioning seriously clouds the clinical picture and seriously compromises the patient's ability to make use of what goes on in the sessions.

The chronic depression reported by the patient may be

found to be “cured” when the person has stopped the use of alcohol (which is a depressant) and has been off it long enough to be thoroughly detoxified. I will tell the alcohol-abusing patient that it makes no sense for me to spend years trying to analyze his depression when it may be little more than a side effect of the alcohol. I say it will be a waste of my time and his money. I say that the probability of psychotherapy helping him or her is close to zero if not zero. This, of course, constitutes a confrontation. Substance abuse is a situation that calls for such confrontation. I suggest Alcoholics Anonymous to some individuals.

One woman reported symptoms that sounded like borderline dissociative experiences. When free of alcohol and marijuana, both of which she had used heavily every night for years, the borderline symptoms disappeared. There certainly was significant narcissistic pathology, but there was a much more cohesive self-organization than there appeared to be when she was still using.

It is worthwhile to have a short exploratory period in which confrontation and exploration of the resistances to giving up the substance are undertaken. However, in my own practice, if it does not seem likely that a sober alliance will develop in rather short order, I will decline the continuation of treatment. A safe frame is also a sober frame.

## ANONYMITY

The anonymity of the therapist is an aspect of the frame, insofar as its absence introduces actual perceptions or awarenesses that impact on the patient in an intrusive way. A photograph of the therapist’s wife on his desk may evoke responses that can be considered “grist for the mill,” as indeed they may be. However, it may also evoke certain feelings prematurely as well as precluding the emergence of fantasies that would be important to the analytic work. We cannot avoid revealing ourselves to some degree. We reveal ourselves in many ways, and the way we dress, carry ourselves, and furnish our consultation room speaks to who we are. So, shall we then work in a stark room of ivory-painted walls, with no pictures or books, with only a clock to decorate the wall or table? Some therapists believe that having a box of Kleenex in the room is a departure from neutrality and thus a violation of the frame, that it goes too much in the direction of gratifying a wish. And what does *not* having a box of Kleenex say and do? The inevitable expression of our humanness can be viewed as a manifestation of the "shape" of the therapist, and if the patient responds to it, we try to understand that reaction as part of the analytic process.

What is important is to understand the purpose of the frame: to maintain an arena of safety for both patient and therapist and to keep out elements that will unnecessarily intensify, complicate, contaminate, or conceal the transference. It protects the analytic work from stimuli that would prove to be antianalytic in their impact.

## THE FRAME AND THE THERAPIST'S SELF-DISCLOSURE

Psychoanalysis as a clinical theory (a theory of treatment) has come a long way, from the concept of the analyst as a blank screen upon which the patient projects his intrapsychic realities to the concept of psychotherapy as an interpersonal process. We now hear self psychologists speak of the role of the therapist as a selfobject who opens the path of empathy between self and selfobjects (see Chapter 5, p. 61). Others are like Grunes (1984), who refers to the "therapeutic object relationship." Speaking of structural impairment "which cannot be met by interpretation alone" (p. 123), he asks,

> Could the analyst's developmentally informed input, as at least a semi-real figure, reverse serious structural distortions, or even develop parent-like forms of psychic provision which would ultimately fill in aspects of missing structure? [p. 125]

From Grunes' perspective, the therapist is more than a blank screen, more than a functional selfobject. He emphasizes both the real and the illusional aspect of that therapeutic relationship. Although the therapist does not talk about himself or herself, something real about the therapist also comes through and has an impact on the patient. One woman, responding to what she called her therapist's "warm presence," suddenly gained access to the pain of the bleakness of the absence of that kind of warm presence vis-à-vis her mother and others in her family. Only when she experienced it interpersonally with her therapist, could she tolerate the pain of not having had it and could she come to realize the impact of this emotional impoverishment on her subsequent development. Elsewhere (1984) I have referred to the importance of the interpersonal therapeutic matrix in the emergence of the self.

The question will surely arise, no matter which of these particular theories may be guiding the therapist as to if, when, and how much the therapist should reveal about his or her own life details, history, or current feelings in the immediacy of the therapeutic moment. If anonymity protects the frame, is there any room for self-disclosure? Little

(1990) reveals that Winnicott would answer questions truthfully unless there was a need to protect another person.

> He would answer questions directly, taking them at face value, and only then considering (always with himself, often with the patient) why was it asked? Why then? And what was the unconscious anxiety behind it? [p. 47]

When there is an impulse or readiness on the part of the therapist to disclose something personal, he or she should hold back long enough to wonder about the motivation to do so. There may be a clinically sound reason for it. However, even then, it is wise subsequently to wonder with the patient about the effect of that self-disclosure on him or her. Often such disclosure will be a manifestation of an acting out in response to some felt countertransference discomfort, but not always.

## THE NARCISSISTIC PATIENT

The more narcissistic the patient, the greater the patient's need to regard the therapist as a selfobject, as a quasi-extension of the self either representationally or functionally. The therapist may, under these circumstances, experience a kind of "existential annihilation." For all practical purposes, his separate and unique self is disregarded. Self-disclosure may be an unconscious attempt on the part of the therapist to reassure himself that he does, indeed, still exist. There may be an unconscious resentment of that annihilation. The greater the narcissistic pathology of the patient, on the other hand, the more likely the chance that he or she will experience the therapist's introduction of material about himself as an intrusion or abandonment.

## RESPONSE TO PROJECTIVE IDENTIFICATION

As described in Chapter 4, the countertransference reactions to the patient's use of projective identification can be extremely disconcerting, and even disorienting at times. Whether to contain the projection—to hold it, as it were, without *becoming* it—or whether to give it back to the patient through interpretation is a clinical decision. Sometimes the "giving it back" (Tansey and Burke 1989, p. 99) may entail disclosing to the patient the effect the projection has had on the therapist. Whether this is done will be determined by the patient's capacity to stand back and look at the process from that vantage point at the moment. The therapist's self-disclosure with respect to his or her emotional state may be experienced by the patient as accusatory and blaming rather than analytically useful. Indeed, there may be times when the disclosure actually does speak to the therapist's anger at what the patient "has done to him."

## THE HUMANISTIC ENCOUNTER

Therapists who value the humanistic goal of the I–Thou encounter, which was described by Martin Buber (Friedman 1976), seek to make this kind of encounter possible in the treatment situation. In the I–Thou relationship, each person's whole being must be involved. This entails genuine listening to the other without prejudgment about the person who is speaking. There are some humanistic psychologists who see in this goal an indication to self-disclose as part of the treatment. Unfortunately, this may backfire with many patients who may feel, for example, unsafe, assaulted, abandoned, annihilated, or overridden. They may react with a variety of defenses, including emotional withdrawal or passive submission. Obviously, this is not a situation that will predispose to a genuine I–Thou encounter. This would be a situation, then, in which the *goal* of treatment – that is, the capacity to have an I–Thou encounter – is misinterpreted and used as a rationale for injudicious self-disclosure on the part of the therapist. Humanistic–existential treatment *goals* can be facilitated by an understanding of the concepts of character structure and its implications for the treatment process.

The more the therapist reveals about himself or herself, the more likely it is that a reaction to it will be evoked in the patient. Although this reaction may be useful to understand, it is also possible that the patient's self-exploration will be derailed for the time being.

Self-disclosure may be elected when a patient wants to know something personal about the therapist. Although the ideal course is to inquire as to what concern stands behind the question, there are times when at least some minimal reply is indicated insofar as a refusal will be unduly wounding to the patient. Very often such questions are matters that are of public knowledge anyway, such as whether the therapist is married. Minimal self-disclosure would be a simple yes or no. In this situation, further inquiry as to the patient's reaction to that information is important, as it is sure to have some impact. The patient will be better able to explore the concern behind the question at this point and the treatment will not be derailed by what may be experienced as an unwinnable power struggle by the patient.

When one *does* choose to reveal something personal for a thought-out purpose, and when we then check into the patient's reactions to that communication, we will want to see what he or she has done with the process as well as with the content. One can say something like, "I wonder what your reaction was to my telling you that?" The timing of this question would be important, since one would not want its premature formulation to interfere with what the self-disclosure was meant to accomplish in the first place. We may be surprised that it did not lead to what might have been expected. This is an example of not taking for granted that we know what is going on. Joseph (1985) reminds us that "everything that the analyst is or says is likely to be responded to according to the patient's own psychic make-up, rather than the analyst's intentions and the meaning he gives to his interpretations" (p. 453). This is certainly true with respect to the therapist's self-disclosure.

One might self-disclose with the notion that it will make the patient feel less abnormal, that you, his therapist, once had the same kinds of feelings or concerns. This could backfire if instead of communicating empathy—the capacity to know what the patient is feeling and that it is OK—the patient is upset because it disturbs his idealization of you, an idealization that is still needed to make him feel you are reliable and he is safe. There may be both good and bad news with respect to the therapist's departure from anonymity. One has to decide whether the positive outweighs the negative and whether the negative can be usefully resolved.

If one general theme, one guiding principle can be drawn, it is that every clinical decision must be made on the basis of the therapist's understanding of *this unique individual.* Students ask me what to do if the patient wants to give them a gift. The answer will be a question: what will be the consequences of accepting the gift and what will be the consequences of refusing it? Refusal of a gift that is an expression of the patient's genuine gratitude can be devastating, not unlike the effect on a child of the mother's rejection of its offer of love. If refusal of a gift will be so narcissistically wounding that the therapeutic alliance will be damaged, it is better to receive it with a simple thank you and to hold off until a later date addressing the issue. I worked with one man who believed that people only liked him because of what he did for them. For the first two Christmases he bought me expensive gifts. I was absolutely sure that he would equate the refusal of the gift as a refusal of him, as he would also have experienced my interpretation at that time. We worked on the need to pay his way and the wish not to be "beholden" until he was able to stop playing this out in his outside life. He came to realize that I cared for him beyond the money I made from his fee. At that point, he simply stopped bringing me gifts. I did not feel it necessary to go back and bring up the earlier gifts because at that time it would have been experienced as a humiliation.

I recall two times I did refuse gifts: one was an obvious attempt to bribe me into not being angry at the patient because she was taking a trip the next week and would be missing our session. I said no thank you and made the interpretation, and it proved well that I did. The other occasion was with a very disturbed man always on the brink of a psychotic transference. An obviously expensive gift was delivered to me. I didn't open it, but simply said it was a matter of policy not to accept gifts from patients. I believed that this statement of frame was necessary as a reinforcement of reality. The narcissistically vulnerable individual needs to feel special but in the absence of loss of reality testing is likely to feel wounded by this statement of frame. Each situation has to be considered individually in the context of whether the patient is ready to look at the need to be special in an analytic fashion. If there is no such readiness and the confrontation would be wounding, the alliance could be damaged.

When the answer is still uncertain, I ask myself which of the two possible errors—interpreting when I shouldn't or not interpreting when I should—is least likely to harm. The work can always be done later when the patient's observing ego and capacity to endure disappointment are felt to be more securely grounded.

# CHAPTER 9

# Resistance

## RESISTANCE AND DEFENSE MECHANISMS

Resistance is perhaps an unfortunate term for the manifestation of defense mechanisms or character defenses in the treatment situation. From the patient's unconscious, or at times conscious, point of view, these defenses protect the self from a variety of intrapsychic or interpersonal dangers. As long as they are in play, the process of exploration and discovery comes to a halt—which is where the word resistance comes in. It is not a bad habit to be done away with, but a defense to be understood and its important function carefully analyzed. Articulation of the *danger* behind the defense in time should enable the individual to relinquish it. In a similar manner, articulation of unconscious wishes that are embedded in the resistance is necessary for its resolution.

## RESISTANCE TO THE TRANSFERENCE

The concept of *resistance to the transference* implies a warding off of a manner of relating that is both wished for and feared by the patient. For example, a resistance to a dependent transference may imply deep dependency yearnings alongside anxiety at the vulnerability and danger inherent in depending on anyone. Such a patient may insist that the therapist is a person of little consequence, that it is strictly a business arrangement, denying the interpersonal aspect of the process that is at the very heart of analytic therapy.

Sometimes patients are aware that if they allow themselves to rely on the therapist in any form, they are sure to be disappointed sooner or later. They are also aware that such disappointment will be followed by intense anger that will quite probably destroy the relationship if not, as their unconscious fear believes, the therapist himself or herself. The resistance to the transference is thus aimed at preserving the therapist and/or the relationship. This defense creates a paradox and a clinical impasse inasmuch as the relationship must be denied in order to preserve it. Sometimes a great deal of preparatory work must be done before the patient's dilemma can be directly confronted. If the interpretation is premature, the patient may experience it as coming from the therapist's need for involvement rather than from concern for the patient or for the therapeutic process.

It may be only the therapist's uncomfortable awareness of being held off at a distance, at being annihilated at one level, of feeling invisible, that will alert to the possibility of a resistance to the transference. A clear understanding of what such a resistance might mean in terms of the underlying character structure and dynamic conflicts will inform the therapist as to the appropriate handling or interpretation of the resistance. Interpretation, when made, should carry with it an empathic recognition of the survival value of the defense so that the patient does not feel blamed or unnecessarily pathologized. For example, one might say something like, "I fully understand and appreciate the necessity of making me not be—that right now your sense of survival as a self is what is most important. Even though you have had to pay a price for your self-protection, your determination to survive has carried you through many difficult years. Now, because of the loneliness that goes with the defense, you wish for something different, but are afraid to let down the protective walls." The gradual buildup of a sense of safety in the therapeutic relationship prepares the way for such an interpretation and makes it possible for the patient to relinquish the costly self-protection.

## TRANSFERENCE RESISTANCE

*Transference resistance* refers to a defensive mode of relating to the therapist and can be viewed as the patient's way of managing the therapeutic relationship so as to bring about a wished for and/or prevent a feared interaction with the therapist. This may come out of the anxiety of neurotic conflict or out of the dictates of character pathology.

J. Sandler (1981) notes that fulfillment of unconscious wishes entails a reactivation of a particular interaction between inner representations of the self and the object. When such a reactivation and wish fulfillment is actualized in the therapeutic relationship—a process that is at times quite subtle and clinically invisible—the necessary work of the analysis is not done.

One especially difficult-to-perceive transference resistance is one in which being sick (and by derivative, being a patient) is in fact an acting out of a special relationship with the mother that revolved around the patient's being ill and needing her care. This way of being fits in with the concept of the false self (Winnicott 1965), with the "sick" identity being evolved both as a way to be close to mother and as a way to protect the true healthy self from impingement or rejection. At the same time, such a stance allows for oedipal triumph, a way to gain specialness with mother, and at the same time, because of the impotence that goes with being "sick," it defends against incestuous dangers. All of these complexities may be acted out by the very act of being in treatment. In effect, the wish for treatment is a *symptom*. In such a situation, the therapist is simply co-opted into the neurosis. One man with such a dynamic sought out sex therapists for treatment for his "sexual problems" as a way to have sexual satisfaction without anxiety or guilt. Obviously, the therapist's ability to recognize this complex dynamic and to interpret it will be necessary to prevent the evolution of an interminable treatment.

A self-effacing, compliant, or placating attitude toward the therapist is another manifestation of transference resistance—a situation in which defensive postures are enacted in the therapeutic relationship. The following exchange is an example.

P. I sensed you were angry with me last time because I didn't give you what you wanted about the feelings in my dream. I could tell by your voice.

T. (Very sure this was a misperception) I don't know what my voice was like, but what is important is how you interpreted what you perceived.

P. I was aware of trying to please you, so I tried harder.

T. I wonder if these concerns have shaped how you've been with me all along.

P. Sure. I don't know what to do in this room. I look for messages.

It is obvious that such a self-protective stance would interfere with the emergence of material that is critical to the treatment. In fact this patient added:

P. I'm afraid that I won't want to show the feelings you are trying to get to. I don't even know if there is anything there. I was raised in a permissive household with leashes, emotional and physical.

The opening up of the resistance to exploration resulted in the emergence of important family dynamics material and in the revelation that both parents clearly said he should not reveal his feelings to people, that showing feelings is a sign of weakness. The patient commented, "Any wonder things are weird in the world."

Another common transference resistance that is at times difficult to separate out from the overall process is an idealization of the therapist that is embedded in the idealization of psychoanalysis or psychotherapy itself. Such idealizations are derivative of either primitive preoedipal idealizations of the powerful primary object or of the idealized oedipal father. The analysis of women by male therapists is often encumbered by the latter, and more often than not, not only is the therapist unaware of the problem as a transference resistance but he is also unconsciously gratified by it. A sometimes sycophantish adulation of the founding fathers (and mothers) of psychoanalysis, and by derivative, its teachers and practitioners, stands as a formidable transference resistance. Its interpretation may confront the analyst with his or her own need to maintain such idealizations and to identify with the idealized figures.

## RESISTANCE TO TERMINATION

Another manifestation of the idealization of the treatment itself that may lead to an interminable process is the situation in which patients bring characterologically entrenched feelings of inferiority to the work. There may be a belief that with enough analysis there will be a magical undoing of the past in which they felt, by virtue of social class perhaps, or education or achievement, less than certain others who were held up to them as idols. Not infrequently, these others were wealthy, successful, or eminent relatives. The fantasy of a magical undoing necessitates the maintenance of the idealization of therapy; otherwise, they are, in their minds, doomed by their history. The resolution of this transference is essential to a possibility of termination of treatment.

Another transference resistance that makes termination impossible is guilt or anxiety at overthrowing the authority of the parental figure. This may be accompanied by resentment or envy or covert rebellion. Loewald (1979) notes that this overthrow of parental authority and the assumption of responsibility for one's own life takes place developmentally along with the severing of the dependent ties of childhood. Loewald says,

> Not only parental authority is destroyed by wresting authority from the parents and taking it over, but the parents, if the process were thoroughly carried out, are being destroyed as libidinal objects as well. . . . [p. 757]

The wish to preserve or protect the parental figures will be manifest in treatment as well, and the idealization of the authority of the therapist will go unchallenged. The final step in the resolution of the Oedipus complex and the negotiation of the developmental tasks of adolescence necessitate this shift, as does a fully worked through termination phase in treatment.

The resistance to ending may come from a wish to avoid feelings of loss, sadness, and grief, and the work of mourning is essential to the termination process. Early experiences of loss and unresolved grief will intensify this particular resistance.

## RESISTANCES DUE TO INTRAPSYCHIC CONFLICT

Defenses against the emergence of conflictual material, of anxiety-ridden memories, of guilty wishes, or of feelings that jeopardize a precious image of the self, are also resistances that must be identified, interpreted, and resolved. With the increasing public sanction of admissions of early sexual abuse, such material is coming to the fore more and more frequently. Even so, the resistance to remembering is formidable, inasmuch as the memories evoke such terrible shame as well as fear and guilt. Only the patient's trust in the therapist as accepting, nonjudgmental or nonpunitive, and as a safe confidant will make the full working through of this kind of early emotional trauma possible.

## RESISTANCES THAT PROTECT STRUCTURAL VULNERABILITY

A young woman habitually came to her weekly session half an hour late. As we came to understand it, the 30-minute separation between the time I expected her and the time she actually came was necessary to her sense of having a boundary, of knowing whether she was coming for me or coming for herself. Another patient found interpretations intolerable as he could not tell whether they came from the therapist's mind or his own.

In both of these examples, being late or rejection of interpretations even though they were true, the resistance was necessary to the patient's sense of his or her very existence. Interpretation is necessary as a means of bringing the issues into conscious awareness, although interpretation may not be enough to enable the patient to give up the resistance (i.e., the defense). Sometimes it takes time for the developing relationship and the increasing structuralization of the ego to enable relinquishing them. When the therapist takes these defenses personally or misinterprets them as a sign of anger and so interprets them, the patient may become frightened and intensify his or her defensive posture.

## RESISTANCES THAT DEFEND AGAINST POTENTIAL LOSS

J. Sandler (1990) notes that "one source of severe resistance in analysis, which often leads to a negative therapeutic reaction, is our need to cling to the internal objects we have constructed" (pp. 878–879). The negative therapeutic reaction refers to those situations in which the analytic work itself, particularly if apparently successful, creates anxiety or depression, or some other manifestation of loss of progress. This does not refer to situations of therapeutic error, but to instances in which change itself carries an unconscious threat. One woman noted that if she gave up the pathological tie to her mother, who used the daughter as a receptacle for her projective identifications, she would have nothing left, only blackness and emptiness.

The fear of change and loss has to be understood and specifically worked with to free the individual from being held hostage to the internal object. The therapeutic relationship and the gradual attachment to and internalization of the good-enough therapist will enable such a patient to give up clinging to the internal object and to establish more mature and gratifying interpersonal relationships.

By and large, with the uncovering, interpretation, working through, and resolution of the resistances, the major part of the analytic task is done. At this point, the patient is freer to evolve a new view of the self in relationships and in the world, to use resources that have been compromised, and to create new goals, values, and purpose in life.

# CHAPTER 10

# Character Structure and Diagnosis

A developmental-structural model and approach to diagnosis is most useful insofar as it carries with it information as to what is required from treatment to enable growth or cure. This stands in contrast to the medical model in which diagnoses are based on clusters of symptoms.

A useful way to think about the individual *diagnostically* is to assess ego and superego functions—that is, to establish a picture of how the individual's psyche is organized (i.e., structured).

This will give information as to relative strengths and weaknesses of the personality.

Character structure refers to the overall organization of the personality—the specifics of that organization for a given individual. This includes object relations (Chapter 7) and the nature of the inner representational world, but it also takes into account the organization of all other aspects of ego functioning as well. It is more like an x-ray than a photograph and as such is useful in the making of clinical decisions.

## THE EGO FUNCTIONS

From an ego psychological viewpoint, the ego is defined in terms of mental functions, and when we speak of the relative health or weakness of the ego, we refer to the organization of these functions, particularly in terms of their integration. Ego is not a synonym for "self" or "self-esteem" (as in the vernacular, "He sure has a big ego!").

The ego functions are: (1) relation to reality, (2) regulation and control of instinctual drives (sex and aggression), (3) thought processes, (4) defense mechanisms, (5) autonomous functions, (6) synthetic function, and (7) object relations.

Of all of these, object relations—the internally organized, structured images of the self and the primary caretaker—can be seen as the set *within which* the other functions of the ego must be integrated, particularly into and within the self representation (the internal self-structure). For example, are the feelings and impulses experienced as part of the self (integrated) or do they simply erupt without a cognitive content to bind them and render them understandable? This final umbrella formulation is central to a view of the individual as more or less integrated and thus as more or less psychologically healthy. Object relations theory is especially useful because of its explanatory potential with respect to the psychological integration of the separate functions of the ego within a psychological self.

The character structure also entails the nature of the superego. This includes the qualities of conscience and the qualities of the ego-ideal.

## ASSESSMENT

The following approach to assessment is essentially an operational approach – a way to derive the formulation from the diagnostic interview itself.

### Relation to reality

1. *Reality testing* refers to the patient's capacity to distinguish between wishes and/or fears and reality.

2. *The sense of self as real* indicates that the individual experiences the self as real most of the time, allowing for the use of depersonalization as a defense under stress.

3. *The ability to look at the self objectively* enables the person to stand back and ally himself or herself with the interviewer to explore the patient's wishes, feelings, beliefs, and actions. This is what is also referred to as the *observing ego*. In treatment, when there is a disruption or loss of the observing ego, restoring it is the first order of business. This is usually done by tending to the source of the disruption itself. The presence of an observing ego, at least a good part

of the time, is a prerequisite for doing the work of a dynamic psychotherapy.

**Regulation and Control of the Instinctual Drives**

When we speak of the instinctual drives, we refer to sex and aggression. They are instinctual insofar as they are at least in part biologically influenced, although in humans their expression is shaped in accordance with psychological as well as biological principles. An instinct theory is one that views sex and aggression as the prime movers, as the experiences that comprise the *organizing principle* for mental behavior. An ego psychology or object relations approach to these drives considers them simply as one aspect of human experience that has to be integrated within the overall psychic organization of the self along with other aspects of experience. Whatever our theoretical attitude toward these drives, or impulses, our assessment procedure should take them into account.

1. *The capacity for delay* refers to the individual's ability to tolerate the frustration of wishes in general, and of these drives in particular. In the interview we can observe the individual's ability to accept the demands of the intake process and to delay expression of pressing feelings or wishes.

2. *Adequate impulse control* is indicated by the individual's ability to talk about sexual or aggressive impulses without having to discharge them into action.

3. *The capacity for adaptive expression* means that the control of sexual and aggressive impulses is not too rigid to allow for their appropriate expression in reality and freedom to discuss them in the interview.

## Thought Processes

*The ability to think conceptually and logically* will be evident in the interview. We also want to take into account cognitive issues, such as a tendency to think categorically, in black and white terms, or any disruption of the thought processes under emotional stress or psychological conflict. We will also look at the capacity for abstract thinking or a tendency to be concrete. The thought processes are susceptible to interference from psychological causes in spite of a constitutionally good mind. Serious thought disorders are indicative of severe psychopathology. When signs of a thought disorder are extremely subtle, the therapist may feel puzzled as to why it is so difficult to follow the patient's thinking.

There are some therapists who neglect or eschew the cognitive work of the treatment process, equating it with the defense mechanism of intellectualization. Nothing can be further from the truth. The schemata of self and other, the mental representations of internalized interpersonal relationships are *cognitive structures,* albeit characterized by associated affective and motivational forces. It is the cognitive structure that binds and structures affect and gives it meaning. Belief systems based on malevolent relationships are cognitive systems, and need exploring in their own right.

These belief systems are built up in the early years by the child in its attempts to make sense of its experience. For example, the child who experiences repeated feelings of abandonment because the mother has to go to work every day and leaves the child with nonfamiliar caretakers, may come to believe that mother does not stay with him or her because he or she is bad or not worth very much. In therapy, an exploration of the feelings of abandonment alone does not help the patient's sense of hopelessness about ever having a good relationship. It is the long-established belief system concerning the child's worthlessness that generates in the here and now an ongoing sense of hopelessness. This belief system must be highlighted in terms of both its origins and its present consequences. At this point, the individual is able to let in new interpersonal experience that contradicts the deeply held beliefs about himself.

Cognition is one of the basic, innate capacities of the human brain. It is a resource we count on in the treatment process. As a basic tool, attention to disordered cognition must be attended to first and foremost. An example of this would be the exploration of the defensive nature of categorical thinking (e.g., the need for certainty). Attention to the cognitive dimension of mental functioning is a sine qua non for structural change.

## Defenses

An essential concept of psychoanalytic theory is that of intrapsychic conflict that generates anxiety and the elaboration of defenses against that anxiety. These defenses include repression, regression, reaction-formation, isolation, undoing, denial, projection, introjection, turning against the self, and reversal. Anna Freud (1946) suggests that sublimation also be viewed as a defense, although sublimation pertains rather to the study of the normal than to neurosis.

> Sublimation, i.e., the displacement of the instinctual aim in conformity with higher social values, presupposes the acceptance or at least the knowledge of such values, that is to say, presupposes the existence of the super-ego. [p. 56]

Early analytic theory describes the defenses in terms of drives and the relationships among the id, the ego, and the superego. If we take the perspective of the development of the self as structure within a relational context, we can describe defenses relative to this process and structure. For example, we can note that because of the failure of the primary caretaker during the early rapprochement period, the child fell back on its primitive omnipotence to build up the pathological grandiose self as a defensive structure. Thus, we now have the concept of defensive *structures* as well as defense mechanisms.

The defense mechanisms are automatic mental mechanisms that protect the individual from psychological stress, whether this stress is evoked internally or by external factors. Everyone uses certain defense mechanisms. We want to know if they do what they are intended to do and if there are detrimental side effects from the use of these mechanisms. Sometimes certain defenses are adaptive (useful) in early childhood, but become maladaptive in adult life.

1. *The adequacy* of the defenses is indicated by the patient's ability to tolerate negative and positive affect (anxiety, depression, guilt, shame, anger, love, affection, pleasure); by his or her ability to talk about both negative and positive feelings; and the ability to recover readily from a regressive reaction and talk about it.

2. *The flexibility* of the defenses is indicated by the person's ability to examine the defenses themselves in the interview.

3. *The maturity* of the defenses refers to the developmental level with which they are associated, this level being in part determined by the quality of both cognitive and emotional development when they first arose as defenses.

The more advanced defenses are intellectualization,

sublimation, repression, rationalization, or displacement. Each of these requires relatively mature mental, intellectual capacities. Repression as a defense mechanism may be considered a motivated forgetting. This stands in contrast to primal repression, the inability to remember the earliest stages of life before there was language and a way to organize experience cognitively so that it was rememberable. Repression as a defense implies, at least at some level, an awareness that what is repressed is associated with psychological pain. There is an active, albeit unconscious, decision not to be aware of it. Repression does not deny reality. It is a refusal to be consciously aware of it.

Sublimation requires the development of a mature relation to the external world that offers productive channels through which certain feelings and impulses can be expressed without doing violence to the psychological self. A need to control can be channeled into an occupation that allows for expression of that need in a way that is emotionally distinct from the original defensive need to control.

The more primitive modes of defense are projection, externalization, somatization, denial, or introjection. Projection and introjection are associated with too permeable boundaries of the self, a partial loss of differentiation of self from other. This is a mental state associated with early mental and emotional development. Denial is different from repression in that it requires a distortion of reality, a not knowing what one does know. It has an omnipotent, magical thinking quality to it, a belief that "if I say it isn't true, it isn't true." Such magical thinking is associated with early childhood, and thus denial is classified as a more primitive defense.

### The Autonomous Functions

The autonomous functions are those mental operations that are innate and constitutionally based and that develop in accord with a maturational timetable. Hartmann (1939) writes:

> Not every adaptation to the environment, or every learning and maturation process, is a conflict. I refer to the development *outside of conflict* of perception, intention, object comprehension, thinking, language, recall-phenomena, productivity, to the well-known phases of motor development, grasping, crawling, walking, and to the maturation and learning processes implicit in these and many others. [p. 8]

While these various functions arise by virtue of innate genetic, neurological, and constitutional forces—those that are essentially "hard-wired"—they can be caught up in conflict, and their smooth unfolding can be derailed in one way or another. Stuttering is an example of a symptom that may develop when the innate ability to develop speech becomes fraught with conflict and anxiety. Hartmann notes that it would

> be useful to distinguish three kinds of developmental processes: those which occur without any essential and specific influence of the external world; those which are coordinated to typical experience (that is, which are triggered by average expectable environmental situations . . .); and finally, those which depend upon atypical experiences. [pp. 103–104]

In assessing the relative health or pathology of the autonomous functions we note the following.

1. *A relative independence from conflict* means that speech, cognition, perception, or motor behavior are not impaired in life or in the interview because of psychological reasons.

2. *Recoverability* implies that if the autonomous func-

tions are partially impaired, this can be understood and worked with in a psychological context by the patient.

3. *Organic integrity* means that there are no neurological disorders that would cause impairment that interfered with the ability to do the work of the interview.

## Synthetic Functions

The synthetic function of the mind refers to the inherent ability of the brain to do the work of organizing experience. While it is actually one of the autonomous functions, it is important to look at it independently insofar as it directly relates to the individual's capacity to make use of the analytic treatment process.

1. *Psychological mindedness* refers to the individual's ability to think in terms of psychological cause and effect.

2. *The capacity for insight* means that the person is able to draw valid psychological conclusions with respect to his or her own feelings, wishes, thoughts, and behavior.

Together with the availability of an observing ego, these abilities are essential for doing the work of a dynamic psychotherapy.

## Object Relations

Chapter 3 contains a more elaborate discussion of the stages of object relations development. An in-depth understanding of how the person functions as a psychological being with an identity and capacity for relating to others is based on this greater in-depth understanding. The items included here are based on observations made during the individual interview and do relate to the developmental stages and processes described in Chapter 3.

1. *Basic trust* can be determined to be present if the person is able to see at least one person as benign and trustworthy. The ability to make use of the relationship with the therapist will require this capacity. A satisfactory symbiosis in the earliest months of life leads to this basic trust.

2. *Relatedness* is indicated by the patient's capacity to be emotionally present and interpersonally engaged during the interview. Significant detachment, on the other hand, suggests a strong need to defend against relatedness because it is felt to carry some kind of danger. This danger may pertain to any one of the several stages of hierarchical development.

3. *Differentiation* refers to the ability to perceive the interviewer and others as separate and different from the self. An adequate negotiation of the separation-individuation process is necessary for this ability.

4. *Stability* of object relations tells us that the patient can work with transference interpretations without losing a realistic perception of the interviewer. This may be missing in certain more primitively organized patients, in which case making transference interpretations, at least in the early phase of treatment, will be contraindicated. The individual has to be able to tolerate the fact that the therapist has an existence separate from his or her own. An intermediate goal of treatment would be to bring the patient to the point where he or she can tolerate the more demanding level of work.

5. *Integration* of object relations is measured by the patient's ability to tolerate ambivalence toward himself and others. That is, there is no split between disparate images of the self and disparate images of the object.

6. *Maturity* of object relations is evident in the person's ability to establish and maintain true peer relationships and in the capacity for altruism. When there is a pathological

degree of narcissism, of self-centeredness and emotional dependency, others are related to on the basis of the individual's own needs or emotional requirements, a situation that precludes the capacity for relating to someone as a peer instead of as a need satisfier, or to be able to be truly altruistic as opposed to using caring and giving as an interpersonal manipulation or form of self-protection.

## SUPEREGO FUNCTIONS

Although the very presence of a superego implies more mature psychological development, what looks like a superego may in fact reflect a more primitive mental and emotional setup. The unassimilated introject of the punitive parent differs from a mature superego, in which the identifications with the parent are felt to be part of the self, rather than as an alien voice within the self as may be the case with the unassimilated introject. An evaluation of the superego in terms of its functions—the conscience and the ego-ideal—is diagnostic of the internal structure, particularly with respect to that of the self and object representations. A healthy superego is derived, in large part, from the internalization of values and standards learned from the parents with whom the child has identified.

### Conscience

1. There are *standards of right and wrong,* and the individual wants to live according to such standards.

2. *The capacity for guilt* is an indication of the person's concern with living up to these standards.

3. These standards should be *realistic,* not requiring unrealistic perfection of morality. The presence of demands

for an unrealistic moral perfection is suggestive of a more primitive organization of the self.

### The Ego-Ideal

The ego-ideal is comprised of more than just rights and wrongs. It is a wider sense of the person one wants to be and is often derived later than the conscience when heroes and models beyond the family begin to have an impact on the young person's life. The earlier roots of a healthy ego-ideal are the parental perception and support of what the child truly values about itself. Feelings of shame or pride are associated with an evaluation of one's self alongside the ego ideal as a standard.

1. *Feelings of worth* indicate that the person has a well-established sense of self as a worthwhile person.
2. The ego-ideal is *realistic* in that the person's self-image does not require unrealistic perfection or reveal grandiosity. These also would suggest a more primitive organization of object relations.

Using the above criteria for assessment purposes gives us a picture of the relative health or pathology of the organization of the psyche, a notion of what kinds of problems we can expect in the treatment process, the kinds of problems that need addressing as part of the treatment process, the healthy resources that can be counted on as part of the working alliance, and the vulnerabilities that must be attended to so as not to traumatize the person as a consequence of the work.

## THE DEVELOPMENTAL-STRUCTURAL DIAGNOSIS

While the above assessment procedure gives information with respect to areas of strength and weakness in terms of ego *functions,* we also need to assess, in particular, the quality of object relations, the organization of the inner representational world. That is, we need to construct a picture of the organization of self and object representations and their associated affects and impulses. We need to know the presence or absence of differentiation of self from other and of the presence or absence of integration of diverse relational schemas. It is these schemas that direct the individual's felt sense of self in the world at large along with patterns of interpersonal relating. These schemas are the outcome of the infant's and small child's organization of repetitive patterns of interpersonal experience into enduring patterns in the mind. These patterns will then be manifest in interpersonal relationships and especially in the transference. We need to know the degree of integration, or absence of it, of the various ego functions within the self representation, and of variations that may exist in this organization. Kernberg (1980), from the same perspective, writes:

> . . . the earliest internalization processes have dyadic features, that is, a self-object polarity, even when self- and object representations are not yet differentiated. By the same token, all future developmental steps also imply dyadic internalizations, that is, internalization not only of an object as an object representation, but of an interaction of the self with the object, which is why I consider units of self- and object representations (and the affect dispositions linking them) the basic building blocks on which further developments of internalized object and self-representations, and later on, the overall tripartite structure (ego, superego, and id), rest. [p. 17]

We have to be careful not to jump to conclusions when the patient's words suggest a developmental disorder, that is, a basic impairment in the organization of the self that requires integration of all the functions of the ego as described in this chapter, and with adequate separation and individuation from the primary object of attachment. The following is an example of how one might be misled by the patient's description of her distress.

> A woman who had been subjected to major traumatic losses and assaults as a child and adolescent—the first occurring when she was 6 years old—told me she was afraid to go to sleep as she was afraid she wouldn't be herself when she woke up in the morning. This statement alone would not be an adequate basis for a structural diagnosis.

Since a child's sense of self and reality is heavily dependent on its environmental surroundings, on an average expectable environment that is predictable and ongoing, traumatic change in that environment may lead to a loss of the sense of the familiar self in a familiar world. Thus, the child is likely to feel, "This isn't me any more!" Normal developmental changes, such as the physical changes of puberty, require a *revised sense* of self, an assimilation of a changed soma into an established psyche. The pubescent adolescent may look at her body and think, "Gee, is this still me?" When traumatic events change the child's world, the child feels changed. Each of us probably experiences everyday variations in our sense of self depending on where we are and whom we are with. When, during childhood, an alcoholic mother who could be both tender and ragefully out of control presents the child with extreme shifts in external reality, the child's sense of the ongoingness of the self is repeatedly disrupted, evoking the experience of existential annihilation. Later in life, people who had been subjected to these traumatic disruptions of the sense of personal ongoingness may reexperience the terrifying annihilation when external or biological experiences again disrupt the sense of self-sameness. If the preoedipal phase of development was good enough to secure a cohesive, differentiated, and integrated self, this is a manifestation of a severe post-traumatic stress disorder rather than of a developmental disorder. They are apprehensively concerned lest the disruption occur once again. They can recall it and talk about it in treatment. It is not simply a state that emerges when the therapist fails in empathy as in the case of the more fragile borderline. These individuals under normal nontraumatizing circumstances have cohesive, differentiated, and integrated selves and are capable of mature relationships. Despite the annihilation anxiety, I do not view them as borderline, although they are sometimes misdiagnosed as such because of the annihilation terror.

Where there is a history of severe trauma, we have to ask, "Who was the child to whom this happened?" Was she a borderline child with structural impairment to start with? Or was her inner organization of self and object adequate and within the normal range?

My patient's capacity to keep functioning despite severe distress spoke to the essential health of her internal organization, as did the quality of her interpersonal relationships. I reassured her that she was not crazy, as she feared, but that her fear was, in effect, a memory of the traumatic changes that confronted her when she was a little girl. I tied the current exacerbation of the anxiety to a here-and-now traumatic event that was changing her external world, the loss of a job where she had made some important friendships.

Recently, the incidence and effects of incest have been given a great deal of deserved attention. However, there seems to be a tendency to lump all incest victims into a single diagnostic group, looking for a single syndrome that would point a finger and say, "Yes, there was incest here." Once again I would emphasize the importance of asking, "Who was the person to whom this happened?" What was the age of the child—at what phase of psychological development did the emotional derailment take place? Was there a cohesive and differentiated self? Was the child well into individuation with an internal good object securely structured? Had the oedipal crisis been negotiated with perhaps only a modicum of residual conflict? Did the incest take place in adolescence, compromising the developmental tasks of adolescence in addition to the impact of trauma and its aftermath? The overall effect on ego functioning will vary according to these and other variables. The presence or absence of physical abuse (separate from the sexual abuse per se), the predominance of affects of hate or love that existed at the time of the incest, and the nature of the incestuous act or acts (e.g., sodomy vs. fondling), as well as the identity of the perpetrator (parent, sibling, or visiting uncle), all will lead to different outcomes. Conflict may be far more intense when the incest was at the hands of a loved father than if at the hands of a feared and hated parent. It is important to understand the impact of the incest in the *unique* case of any one individual. It is also important that we not become so eager to paint a clinical picture of *the* incest victim that we create a pseudoidentity into which every one of them is stuffed, a procrustean bed that will have us treating the label rather than the person. If this becomes a diagnostic entity in a future *Diagnostic and Statistical Manual of Mental Disorders,* this unfortunate probability will be enhanced, moving even further from a psychological model to a medical model. This approach to the understanding and treatment of some psychological problems leads to a most unfortunate loss of clinical precision and usefulness. I have found that even premenstrual syndrome (PMS), a condition that is supposedly only hormonally based, has been almost completely ameliorated after a successful course of psychoanalytic therapy. Although the hormonal effects are experienced, the psychological sequellae are eliminated. It is my opinion that viewing PMS as a biological entity and thus inevitable has been detrimental to the image of women, who can now be seen as inherently unstable, thus justifying continued sex discrimination in the workplace.

# CHAPTER 11

# Developmental Tasks

From the field of general psychology we need to keep in mind the concept of developmental tasks. Although we can look at these tasks from a psychoanalytic perspective, the concept does not come out of psychoanalytic theory itself. Developmental tasks confront the growing child by virtue of his age and the demands made on him for change appropriate to that age. These tasks can be facilitated by a healthy underlying character structure in object relations terms. They can also be interfered with by a preexisting pathological structure. A vulnerable structure from the perspective of the cohesion, differentiation, and integration of the self representation is likely to be stressed further by developmental requirements.

For example: developmental demands of childhood, such as (1) leaving home to go to school, (2) developing peer relations, and (3) developing skills, talents, and intellectual learning, require a healthy self.

If the self is so fragile and still so dependent on the connection with the primary caretaker as a selfobject to maintain the self's cohesion, having to separate to go to school is likely to cause severe separation anxiety, even panic, and the child may be unable to negotiate the task.

If the child is unduly vulnerable to narcissistic wounding because of a tenuously organized self representation, and if he or she has developed pathological defensive structures such as the grandiose self, he or she is not likely to be able to establish satisfactory peer relations, which require the ability to give and take as equals. The very concept of peer-ness will be alien to that child's sense of reality.

The development of the intellect, and of skills and talents, will be compromised if they have lost their conflict-free status. That is, those functions of the mind that develop as the outcome of the neurological maturation of the brain—the "autonomous functions"—can become embroiled in the dynamics of conflict, anxiety, and defense, or embroiled in the dangers and defenses of pathological object relations. When this happens, the child's constitutional givens with respect to talents and intellect will be compromised.

The same sort of situations prevail in adolescence, when certain developmental tasks will confront the boy or girl, making strenuous demands on the internal organization. In particular, the child must (1) integrate bodily changes and the changes of internal experience that result from hormonal changes, (2) integrate sexuality into the capacity for healthy peer relating and intimacy, (3) emancipate further from parents and family, leading to the eventual move out of the family home, (4) develop a more mature philosophy of life, which entails the final steps in the achievement of a mature superego in terms of both conscience and ego ideal, and (5) begin to think in terms of life goals such as a career.

These demands require a healthy preexisting character structure. A fragile structure will be stressed further and even traumatized by these pressures.

I believe that psychotherapy with the adolescent patient should be in concert with the forward developmental thrust. Using the developmental tasks as a focus for the treatment, the barriers to the negotiation of these tasks can be explored. The therapy relationship should not promote regression, since this may be experienced as intolerably shaming and undermining of only tentatively achieved progression.

When we try to understand a patient from a longitudinal point of view, as we learn his or her history, information as to the relative success or failure of the negotiation of the developmental tasks will provide important clues as to the strengths and vulnerabilities of the individual's internal mental structure.

When we are working with an adult who has come to therapy because of a bad reaction to a particular life event, it will help if we think in analogous terms—that is, what demands has this event made on the individual and what does his or her inability to negotiate the crisis imply about the underlying character structure? Life itself inevitably continues to confront the individual with tasks both common and uncommon for one in a particular decade of life.

Does the death of a spouse lead to a severe depression? Does this suggest that the lost partner was especially important as a selfobject because of the narcissistic pathology of the patient?

Does forced retirement lead to a psychotic depression or paranoia because of the attack on a grandiose self that flourished and was given validity through the work role that has now been taken away?

Both of these situations can be viewed as developmental tasks of later life. These may have been individuals who appeared healthy and who functioned well up to the point when new demands stressed the existing structural setup. The fact that they have done so well for so long also points out that certain strengths co-existed with the vulnerabilities, and both have to be taken into consideration when we work with the individual. They will also have to deal with the blow to the self-esteem that is the outcome of the breakdown in the face of these crises, an issue that calls for the utmost concern and tact on the part of the therapist.

# Part III

# Technical Considerations

What we actually do in the treatment situation will, once again, depend on our understanding of the patient. As quickly as possible, we will want to make some formulation to ourselves concerning the relative strengths and vulnerabilities of the individual. For example, we will get a sense of what the person can tolerate with respect to interpretation, whether or not he or she can tolerate a transference interpretation, or whether he or she will feel endangered by it. We will, as quickly as possible, make some formulation with respect to the core issue, the core developmental issue in terms of underlying character structure, of the nature of the person's inner representational world of self and other; not only to let the person know we understand him or her, but also to inform ourselves as to what our task is in the treatment process.

Treatment outcome research (Luborsky et al. 1988) has confirmed that people benefit most from psychotherapy when a therapist correctly identifies their core relationship problem. This makes sense, since the inner representational world is organized around the relationship between the self and the object, and its relative health or pathology will become manifest in interpersonal relationships. That is, what began as interpersonal experiences vis-à-vis the primary caretaker(s) becomes internalized and structured intrapsychically. Then, what is structured intrapsychically becomes manifest once again in the interpersonal setting.

This section will describe a number of interventions intended to further the therapeutic process. Whether one applies them should be with full knowledge of the effect, for better or for worse, on a given patient at a given moment in treatment.

# CHAPTER 12

# Finding the Metaphor

The human mind, from the beginning of life on, creates symbols and attempts to find meaning in its experience. An ongoing task of therapy is to discover that meaning that is often hidden within a metaphor, be it the metaphor of the dream, or the metaphor of obsessive rumination, or even that of compulsive acting out. One must find the abstraction buried within the concreteness of a symptom or within the banality of a patient's daily reportings. To miss the metaphor is to miss the patient.

Following are some examples of the discovery of the metaphor. In some cases, that discovery sets the patient free from unproductive rumination, advancing the treatment in a sometimes dramatic manner.

## THE OBSESSING PATIENT

The patient who is chronically unable to make decisions—whether to live in one city or another, whether to move toward men or toward women (as in female bisexuality), or whether to take food in or throw it out (as in bulimia)—may be caught in a double approach–avoidance conflict associated with a particular developmental phase. When the metaphor is deciphered, the developmental impasse can be confronted and analyzed.

The bisexual female can confront the dilemma of the condensed rapprochement and oedipal conflicts in which to move away from her narcissistic mother will lead to a loss of mother's love, and in which a move toward father will be fraught with disappointment because of his cold indifference.

The bulimic woman can confront her need–fear dilemma with respect to her preoedipal mother who alternately is enticingly promising and frustratingly abandoning, and her seductive oedipal father who is sexually exciting and sexually dangerous.

In another instance, we may find obsessive rumination, not as a characterological defense as in the illustrations above, but associated with particular content. One man went over and over the ending of his marriage and his anger at what he considered an unfair settlement. He would go back and forth, citing his failures in the marriage but then trying to find reasons not to be held accountable for them. After listening to him for awhile, I wondered with him if his focus on the details and his inability to stop thinking about them might not be a metaphor for something more basic about his inner world. The issue seemed to be one of guilt and punishment, and it was quite likely that the preoccupation with the details of the failure of the marriage made external and real something unconscious that he did not have ready access to. This led to a number of early memories concerning his relationship with his mother and how he blamed himself for her illness and eventual death.

## THE COMPULSIVE PATIENT

Repeated compulsive behaviors may seem so minor as to readily invite being overlooked or passed by as the patient simply moves on to something else. The patient may report them with little concern, perhaps even burying the report in other apparently more important content. The very fact of its repetition and its being dystonic enough to report should alert the therapist to its potential metaphorical implications. It helps to stop the patient and to ask for the *specific details* of what he or she experiences at the brief moment of acting out—what is felt and what is thought. It is these details that allow the therapist to point in the direction of the metaphor.

> A man reported his propensity for flirting, which certainly could be understood and reflected as a pleasant and harmless sexual diversion, a source of excitement in an otherwise tense or difficult day. However, since the patient was as troubled by it as he found it enjoyable, I stopped and asked for the details of what the experience was like for him.

It seemed that he wanted to evoke the woman's interest in him, after which he would abruptly end the brief interchange and walk away, leaving her thinking about him and perhaps desiring him.

From these details I wondered about the flirting as a behavioral metaphor for a wish—a wish to have the woman want him more than he wanted her, and wondered about times he had felt at the other end of such a situation. My inquiry led to the opening up of affect-laden memories of his severe separation panics of childhood, material that had not emerged in previous therapies.

In a first interview I will often ask for the individual's earliest memory. This memory will often reveal a metaphor that communicates a central, if not core, object-relational structure and dynamic. This man's memory had been one of such panic, and it now made sense as fitting into a wider dynamic-developmental issue.

## DERIVATIVES

Derivative behaviors—replications and reenactments of early developmental, relational conflicts—are metaphors of a kind. Sometimes it makes clinical sense to work with the derivatives—as with the problems with boyfriends or with bosses—rather than with the original conflict-laden relationships (mother, father, or sibling) or rather than within the transference. However, for the most part, I liken *staying* with the derivatives and avoiding their connection with the past and with the transference to looking in the mirror and attempting to remove a smudge from one's nose by taking a Kleenex and wiping the reflection in the mirror. The metaphorical meaning of the derivative material needs to be interpreted if the core developmental issues are to be addressed.

## THE ADAPTIVE CONTEXT

Some patients will begin a session with casual comments as they walk down the hall or enter the consultation room. They may report some event that had just taken place at work or on the freeway. That is, they chat about everyday realities that, taken at face value, have no meaning that is especially relevant to the treatment process or to the treatment relationship. If one listens for the metaphor that is embedded within this context, one can often find a relationship between these comments and what emerges later in the session, a thread of meaning that connects the reported day-to-day events with therapeutic issues. I may make the connection later in the session, noting the thread that ties it all together. This is especially useful for patients who are not especially psychologically minded, as a way to demonstrate how the mind works with meaning and metaphor, perhaps motivating them to become more interested in that way of thinking and working. Interpretation of the meaning embedded in those opening comments before there is a body of material with which to connect it, may seem arbitrary and "off the wall" to the patient. If one jumps in right away with a comment about those seemingly insignificant statements, the patient's flow of associations is disrupted and the discovery of the significance of the beginning material is likely to be lost. This is a time for the therapist to be patient and not to be clever.

The meaning of content, or the meaning of behavior,

can be approached in a variety of ways. It is all too easy for the therapist to get caught up at the level of what is manifest rather than moving to the meaning that is latent. When this happens, the treatment is likely to be unproductive at best. Every therapist knows how frustrating it is when this happens and how impotent one feels when caught up in the concreteness of the patient's obsessive and perseverative ruminations. The way out for both therapist and patient is through the door of meaning—and the key that unlocks this door is often the buried metaphor.

## DREAMS

The meaning of a dream is often unlocked by the finding of a key metaphor. This is sometimes contained in a single odd element in a dream, something that might make the person wonder why he dreamed of that person or that situation. One woman dreamed of a girl who had been in her elementary school class. Her association to this girl was that she was the smallest child in that class. From there, the implications of "being the smallest" could be explored.

A common dream is that of being unprepared for a high school test or exam. Perhaps the dreamer realizes he had failed to attend class for the entire semester and now is faced with the test. The anxiety may be mitigated by the person telling himself in his dream, "But I already had my master's degree!" As a metaphor, this often stands as the individual's sense of aspects of immaturity, of feeling like a child in an adult world, or of the concomitant sense of inadequacy that comes from using regressive defenses. A not-unusual dream metaphor of individuals who had been the recipient of parental projections is that of overflowing toilets or garbage pails.

Finding meaning in the visual image of the dream is usually accomplished by asking the individual his or her associations to elements of the dream. These associations will generally relate quite clearly to issues that have been coming to the fore in the treatment.

Sometimes the patient will produce rather concrete material that does not seem to go anywhere. He may say, "I don't know why I'm bringing this up." It may be useful to have him make it into a dream, and from the dream metaphor, the meaning of the concrete material can be understood. This entails a conscious construction of the metaphor to find the meaning of the concrete. The dreamer does this for us with his dream.

# CHAPTER 13

# Interventions

The combined goal of inquiry, observation, interpretation, confrontation and integration, is the furthering of the therapy process and with it, the facilitation of the overall goal of that process, be it resolution of conflict, repair of structural deficit, or emotional healing.

## INQUIRY

The purpose of inquiry is to elicit data, not only for our own information, but to deepen and widen the patient's self-awareness. For example, the therapist should never assume he or she understands what the patient means if this meaning is not clear. *Clarification* may be indicated when the material presented has a narrative quality but, in fact, obscures more than it reveals. The use of words that are assumed to have consensual meaning when it is more likely that they have specific meaning for the patient should be clarified. We may assume we know what the patient means when she says she is afraid of rejection. But do we? What does she mean by rejection? What is that experience like for her? The word "upset" is one that is frequently not clarified when, in fact, it may mean angry, afraid, sad, guilty, or ashamed. "What do you mean by 'upset'?" is an appropriate inquiry if the therapist is to be able to understand the patient's experience.

Global statements and generalizations give the appearance of communication, but more often than not tend to be ruminative and unproductive. They invite psychologizing in a manner that carries little or no insight or emotional communication. Asking for specific examples will elicit a deeper level of information and will help the patient deepen the process of self-exploration.

Some examples are as follows:

> P: I think I'm being self-destructive.
>
> T: Can you give me an example of an instance in which you've been self-destructive? What about it felt self-destructive?

or

> P: I'm afraid of rejection.
>
> T: What about it is distressing? Can you give me an example of when you had those feelings?

The inquiry usually communicates the therapist's interest in the patient and in his or her experience and is usually appreciated by the patient.

Other examples of useful inquiry lead to the exploration of the person's fantasies and belief system. For example, the therapist may ask: What did that mean to you? How did you explain that to yourself? Does that remind you of anything that happened in the past? Do you have a reaction to what I just said?

## OBSERVATION

The therapist makes observations of what he or she has noticed when it seems clinically useful, timely, appropriate, and in keeping with what is known about the patient's ability to make use of such observations.

Sequence analysis can take place when the therapist observes to the patient the series of things reported in that session. Simply by noting their associational contiguity, the therapist may then ask, "Do you see a common thread that ties these all together?" Juxtaposing two pieces of data that may have appeared at separate times allows the same sort of "wondering aloud" with the patient. "I wonder if there could be a connection between your feelings of rejection and your detachment. Somehow they seem to go together."

Such observations should be made in a form that allows the patient to defend against the awarenesses that these observations are meant to evoke if that defense is still necessary. Observations should not be made in a way that would make the patient feel objectified or shamed. Comments about the patient's physical nonverbal behaviors must be made judiciously and with sensitivity to the possibility of shame or humiliation. As Langs (1979b) reminds us, "much is conveyed in the tone, style, wording, affective investment, timing, tact, and other verbal and nonverbal qualities of an intervention" (p. 17).

## INTERPRETATION

Langs (1979b) writes that

> *interpretations-reconstructions* allude to the analyst's basic efforts to make unconscious contents, defenses, interactional mechanisms – fantasies, memories, introjects, self and object representations, and the like – conscious for the patient within a dynamic and affective framework. [pp. 15–16]

When we make an interpretation, we bring together islands of awareness, experience, or memory in such a way as to suggest a functional relationship, if not a directly causal one. For example, "You've been telling me how seductive your mother was. I wonder if this doesn't have something to do with your avoidance of sexual relationships now?"

Interpretations are best made in the form of a question, which allows the patient the opportunity to consider the interpretation and to decide if it feels right or not. The interpretation may be right, but the patient may not be ready for it and may reject it. Of course, the interpretation may also not be right, but if the patient does not need to defend against the ideas being explored, he or she might say, "That doesn't really fit, but I think what may be going on is kind of in the same ballpark." The patient will then make what is felt to be the correct interpretation. The more directly our interpretation is drawn from the patient's own behavior and associations, the more sensitive our listening as well as our cognitive understanding of the person, the more likely the interpretation is to be valid and useful for the patient. The patient's response to our intervention, which may take the form of a metaphor, lets us know its impact on him—whether he confirms or rejects the intervention, what new associations it evokes that further the process, or any transferential reactions to our input. When one patient recalled a dream about a house in which the electrical work was being done before the foundation was finished, the therapist noted, "It sounds like you feel I am making connections before you are ready for them."

## INTEGRATION

Integration entails the bringing together of the various islands of new self-awareness, adding the cognitive component that places it all within the overall developmental perspective so that the person's life and experience of it comes to make sense. Disavowed and repressed aspects of the self can be reintegrated with an increasing sense of wholeness and unity of the self.

Examples of integrative interventions are:

> We know that your role as substitute husband for your mother created both anxiety and gratification at being special. We also know that you have been stuck in this role in a way that has not allowed for your developing your manhood, that you have had to sabotage yourself to defend against the dangers of incest as well as to hold on to the gratification of your specialness to her. Your dream tells us that you are ready to relinquish the gratification that has bound you and to leave the role of husband to your father, where it belongs. You're beginning to feel good about your sense of potency and are optimistic about your future.

Another example of an integrative intervention might be:

> You have had to deny your aggression in order to protect an image of yourself as always good. If you were to acknowledge your aggressive impulses, you would have had to give up the moral superiority you claimed over your father. At the same time, if you were able to own your aggression, you would not be caught in the helpless position of victim whose anger takes the form of justifiable and righteous indignation but is not useful for extricating yourself from the passive and helpless position. As you have been able to own those feelings and impulses you were afraid made you bad and deserving of your father's harshness, you find yourself much more effective and unafraid in the world.

Integrative interventions generally follow the uncovering of the various facets of the overall pattern they are meant to elucidate.

## STRUCTURAL AND DYNAMIC ISSUES

The manner in which these several interventions are made will always be guided by one's understanding of the patient's character structure. If there is one idea that bears repeating, it is this, that *all* aspects of the work are to be guided by that understanding. This entails an awareness of the intrapsychic structures of self and other, with an emphasis on both the strengths and vulnerabilities of the self and what may or may not be experienced as endangering to that self by the patient. Empathy entails more than the capacity to feel with the patient and it entails more than listening and intunedness. It also entails a cognitive understanding that enables us to predict our impact on the patient. What will make the person feel safe? What will endanger? What will feel helpful? What will wound? What will feel too close and what will feel too distant? What will feel like interest and what will feel like an intrusion to be warded off?

To some extent we come to these understandings by a certain degree of trial and error at the start of treatment. All five modes of intervention are likely to be used during the intake phase, albeit minimally and tentatively. The patient's responses to our interventions will provide important data about wishes, fears, narcissistic vulnerabilities, and defenses. We will always be guided in the work by what we learn about the patient directly from our interaction with him, a learning process that needs to be tempered with sensitivity and kindness as well as with intelligence. These are all aspects of creating the kind of environment that enables the patient to enter into the therapeutic process with at least a modicum of trust and hope.

## CONFRONTATION

When we confront our patient, we bring something to his attention he may or may not want to see or know. Confrontation runs counter to the defenses. Buie and Adler (1973) define confrontations as

> a technique designed to gain a patient's attention to inner experiences or perceptions of outer reality of which he is conscious or is about to be made conscious. Its specific purpose is to counter resistances to recognizing what is in fact available to awareness or about to be made available through clarification or interpretation. The purpose is not to induce or force change in the patient's attitudes, decisions, or conduct. [p. 127]

As an intervention, confrontation need not be harsh, as is often associated with the word itself. A confrontation can be made with kindness and tact and can be made with concern for its effect on the patient. In fact, as Mann (1973a) notes:

> Gentle, caring concern of the therapist for the patient may well be the most important element of a proper, effective confrontation. [The therapist should communicate] to the patient his privilege to choose the direction that he would like to move in rather than communicating a directive to which the patient feels impelled to yield. [p. 44]

Our understanding of the individual's character structure and the function of the defenses—that is, the nature of the psychic danger being averted by those defenses—will allow us to make the appropriate clinical decision with respect to confronting the defenses.

Buie and Adler (1973) write about the use of confrontation with acting-out borderline patients who put themselves in clear and present danger by that acting out. Acting out refers to the patient's substituting action for verbal communication. Acting-out behavior needs to be understood and interpreted, but when interpretation is insufficient to bring the embedded issues into focus for examination, the therapist may have to set limits against it. They give as an example the case in which the patient, out of rage at what he felt to be his therapist's abandonment, got drunk and purposely drove recklessly, smashing his car. The therapist said

> You could have been hurt, even killed! It was very dangerous for you to do that, and it is important that it does not happen again.

The therapist integrated the confrontation with what was essentially an interpretation as well as reassurance, adding

> The way to avoid danger is to work with your feeling belief that I do not care or do not exist. By all means, whenever you approach believing it, whenever you begin to feel the intense rage which naturally follows, call me up. Call me, talk with me, and that way find out I really do exist, I am not gone. [p. 143]

These writers emphasize the importance of understanding the borderline patient's psychic equilibrium in a way as to be sure that the confrontation does not harm him. As emphasized in this book, they note that the therapist must be aware of the character structure and vulnerabilities of the patient.

## HEROIC CONFRONTATION

Whereas the use of confrontation to a greater or lesser degree is standard to the therapeutic process, Corwin (1973) describes the use of "heroic confrontation" by means of which it is communicated that the patient *must* do something, that is, change in some way within the analysis, or he and the analyst will have to stop their work because it has become nonproductive. This is essentially an emergency situation. Unlike routine confrontation, heroic confrontation *does* make a demand for change on the part of the patient.

I have used such confrontations when it became obvious that the patient's use of substances—alcohol or drugs—was clearly sabotaging the work of treatment. I say without equivocation that it is a waste of our effort, our time, and money to continue unless the person is willing to do what is necessary to stop the use of the particular substance. Heroic confrontation requires a modicum of trust and a good therapeutic alliance. Corwin (1973) writes:

> If no element of love is discernible by the patient, then the confrontation can be taken as proof by the patient that in the end the analyst will be just as cruel, rejecting, demanding, punitive, or unnecessarily harsh as the negative side of the parent in the transference. [p. 85]

In addition, once again, we must keep clearly in mind what the effect of the heroic confrontation will be in terms of the underlying character structure to be sure we do not traumatize the patient. Again, to quote Corwin:

> It should finally be stated that the confrontational manipulation itself should hopefully coincide with a good opportunity of having a positive effect. At the point of the impasse, it is important that the analyst combine his soundest knowledge, his keenest foresight, his greatest empathy, and maximum intuition in a move that can hopefully resolve the impasse, save the therapy, and give the patient the opportunity to free himself from neurotic suffering. [p. 93]

Shapiro (1990) reminds us of the importance of the contextual, interpersonal climate within which our various interventions take place. He writes:

> Imperceptible adjustments in behavior are made to maintain a psychological climate in which observations and interpretations can be utilized. . . . The effect of an interpretation can never be separated from the interpersonal context in which it is given. . . . [Others] stress the impact of the relationship on the interpretation. The content of the interpretation is not a neutral piece of information isolated from the analyst's relationship to the patient. [pp. 501–502]

# CHAPTER 14

# Aspects of the Therapeutic Relationship

The therapeutic relationship can be divided into functional and dynamic aspects and real aspects. It is inevitable that these would become intertwined in the actual work. The increasing focus on psychotherapy as an interpersonal process reveals it to be far more complex than Freud's (1912a) advice that "the doctor should be opaque to his patients and, like a mirror, should show them nothing but what is shown to him" (p. 118). What was reflected back were the transferences through interpretation. He eschews any real interaction with the patient aside from issues of time and money. It is interesting to note Freud's own introductory comment to this chapter.

> I must make it clear that what I am asserting is that this technique is the only one suited to my individuality; I do not venture to deny that a physician quite differently constituted might find himself driven to adopt a different attitude to his patients and to the task before him. [p. 111]

Modern psychoanalysis has come closer and closer to Sullivan's (1940) notion of the process in terms of participant observation. The therapist both affects and is affected by the interpersonal process. However, unlike day-to-day interactions in which most people react on the basis of their own idiosyncratic personality requirements and tendencies (which tends to reinforce and perpetuate the troubled individual's existing pathological internal world of self and object), the therapist mentally steps back to make sense of the overall interaction. He or she then either communicates to the patient this understanding (i.e., makes an interpretation) or uses this understanding as a source of information as to the most helpful course to take at the moment.

Epstein (1982) describes this process as follows:

> At the very least, I think the practice of participant-observation requires us to do the following: that we attempt at all times to study the impact of all possible identifiable factors impinging on the patient's self-system in the crucible of the therapeutic intervention. This means that persistently we shall have to ascertain the positive or negative effects, not only of our interventions, but also of our behavior and of our feelings and attitudes toward the patient and that we need

> always to be prepared to make the necessary adjustments in our continued treatment of him. [pp. 194–195]

The following aspects of the therapeutic relationship are in addition to the transference that is discussed in Chapter 6.

## THE THERAPIST AS SELFOBJECT

The therapist may function as a *selfobject,* in self psychology terms. In so doing, the therapist lends himself or herself to the psychological well-being of the patient in such a way as to help the patient maintain a sense of realness, of cohesion, and of positive self feeling—a process heavily dependent on the empathic sensitivities of the selfobject.[1] It also requires a thorough understanding of the patient's character structure and where the vulnerabilities of the self lie.

## PROVIDING THE HOLDING ENVIRONMENT

The therapist also functions as a provider of *the holding environment.* Winnicott (1960a) describes the function of the holding environment as follows:

---

[1]Individuals who *grow up* playing out this functional aspect of a therapist to their parents develop false-self identities consolidated around the specific idiosyncratic form their character was required to take in order to maintain their parents' well-being and to maintain the connection to them. The true selves of these children tend to be split off with a variety of pathological consequences. These characterological difficulties then confront their own therapists when they seek treatment as adults. They also often become therapists themselves inasmuch as the supportive and quasi-symbiotic role-playing in relationships feels so natural to them. Unfortunately, unless their own therapy frees them from the rigidity of their characterological distortion, they may be impeded in their work with patients. Although the hypertrophied empathic vigilance that was necessary for survival early on often makes them exquisitely sensitive to their patients as well, this will be useful only insofar as their own areas of confusion, conflict, or rigidity are not approached.

> In this place which is characterized by the essential existence of a holding environment, the "inherited potential" is becoming itself a "continuity of being." The alternative to being is reacting, and reacting interrupts being and annihilates. Being and annihilation are the two alternatives. The holding environment therefore has as its main function the reduction to a minimum of impingements to which the infant must react with resultant annihilation of personal being. [p. 47]

Margaret Little (1990), writing of her personal analysis with Winnicott, describes holding in the following terms:

> "Holding," of which "management" was always a part, meant taking full responsibility, supplying whatever ego strength a patient could not find in himself, and withdrawing it gradually as the patient could take over on his own. In other words, providing the "facilitating environment" . . . where it was safe to *be.* [p. 45]

The holding environment provided the patient by the therapist has a function analogous to that of the mother with her infant: to protect the patient's sense of ongoingness of the self from the annihilation experience induced by impingement, providing a place where it is safe to *be.* This holding environment will be facilitated by the maintenance of the safe frame (See Chapter 8). One might say that one of the responsibilities of the selfobject is to maintain the holding environment.

## THE THERAPIST AS CONTAINER

The therapist may also have to function as the *container* of certain aspects of the patient's internal world that are projected into the therapist. Frederickson (1990) notes the difference between being the "repository" and being a container for the patient's projective identifications. In becoming the repository, the therapist replicates the patient's original role in his family. He notes Bion's (1977) concept of containing as follows:

> Containing does not refer merely to holding feelings inside. Containment is the process by which we label those feelings and understand their meaning within the transference. As containers we are not simply passive receptacles; we are active digesters of experience. . . . As containers, we neither deny nor act out our feelings; we digest an initially confusing and overwhelming experience and put it into words. [pp. 491–492]

## THE THERAPIST AS A NEW OBJECT

Greenberg (1986) describes what he calls a relational model of psychoanalysis and the importance of the therapist as a new object. That is, the therapeutic relationship is one within which changes in the self in relation to the object can take place. This is the essence of structural change.

But how can we stand as a new object if we do not offer the alternative of a real relationship as a possibility to the patient whose relationship to us, at the outset, is predominantly shaped by transference?

Grunes (1984) distinguishes what he calls the "therapeutic object relationship" from the real relationship. He cites its relevance to problems of structural impairment that

> combined with the depleted and archaic functioning of external and internal object relations, creates a relationship

> demand factor in treatment which cannot be met by interpretation alone. [p. 123]

And he asks:

> Could the analyst's developmentally informed input, as at least a semi-real figure, reverse serious structural distortions, or even develop parent-like forms of psychic provision which would ultimately fill in aspects of missing structure? [p. 125]

Grunes speaks of the therapist as a semi-real figure, a combination of the illusory and the real.

In his discussion of illusion and narcissism, Mitchell (1986) notes that the analyst must participate in the illusion of existing as the patient's selfobject in order to facilitate the structuralization of a cohesive self. Yet, he also emphasizes that eventually the analyst must also facilitate the dissolution of the illusion in order to establish a richer form of relationship.

What Grunes calls the therapeutic object relationship entails a combination of empathic and cognitive understanding. The first draws us into the patient's affective world; the second anchors us in here-and-now reality.

## THE THERAPIST AS AN OBJECT FOR IDENTIFICATION

Epstein (1982) notes:

> Authenticity is therapeutically relevant only insofar as it becomes internalized by the patient in such a way as to facilitate his progress toward becoming the person he wants

> to be. Among the various features of the therapeutic interaction that might be internalized, the most relevant for facilitating the patient's becoming his most authentic self would be the analyst's therapeutic intentionality. In other words, what I believe becomes internalized by the patient is the analyst's active and persisting struggle both to understand and to meet the patient's therapeutic need. Over the course of [treatment] . . . this aspect of the analyst's behavior becomes translated within the patient into a more active and authentic self-regard. [p. 194]

As a reminder, inappropriate self-disclosure is not what is meant by authenticity. The therapist's authenticity requires his or her full presence and commitment to the moment. Epstein's remarks allude to a dynamic aspect of the relationship, the inevitable identifications with and internalizations of the therapist as a new object. These identifications are analogous the early developmental identifications that are intrinsic to development, both healthy and unhealthy. The therapeutic relationship allows for newer and healthier identifications to take place. However, it is important to be able to recognize the difference between these developmental identifications with the therapist's functions and self-enhancing attitudes and the often-occurring identifications with an idealized therapist that reveal the patient's wish to fuse with his or her idealized object. If the therapist is overly gratified by this idealized identification, he or she may inappropriately reinforce this process.

## THE REAL RELATIONSHIP

Greenson (1967) describes two aspects of what is real in the real relationship between analyst and patient. It may mean

> realistic, reality oriented or undistorted as contrasted to the term "transference" which connotes unrealistic, distorted, and inappropriate. The word may also refer to genuine, authentic, and true in contrast to artificial, synthetic or assumed. [p. 169]

The transference relationship may feel genuine, but it will not be realistic. On the other hand, the working alliance is realistic but it may not feel genuine. Greenson uses the term "real relationship" in reference to that aspect that is both genuine *and* real. He sees the capacity to form a real relationship to the analyst as a prerequisite for analyzability. The empathic response will be experienced as genuine, although what it is in response to may not be realistic. Perhaps it is the genuineness of empathic mirroring that is most significant, inasmuch as it reinforces the patient's sense of genuineness.

Paolino (1982) writes that the real relationship can be distinguished from transference in that "it is relatively less distorted, non-neurotic, appropriate, relevant to the current situation, and not characterized by an indiscriminate duplication of the past . . ." (pp. 231–232). He notes:

> The real relationship is just as important to the psychoanalytic process as the other aspects of the therapeutic relationship. If the real relationship is not actively recognized and utilized in the therapy sessions then the patient is exposed to a relationship with the analyst that is interpersonally sterile and lacking the opportunity for the patient to develop a meaningful and therapeutic object relationship. [p. 232]

Surely Paolino is not talking about the therapist's inappropriate acting out his or her own needs or injudicious self-disclosure. He tells us it is not useful to become analytic automatons rigidly adhering to a notion of proper technique. The flesh-and-blood humanity of the therapist is essential to the aliveness of the process.

Anna Freud (1954) reminds us that in spite of the importance of handling and interpretation of the transference, we should not forget that both analyst and patient are also two real people, of equal adult status, in a real personal relationship to each other. I have heard therapists speak in demeaning ways of their patients because of the presenting pathology. There is no excuse for a lack of respect for the person across from us in the consultation room. At one level or another, we are all "patients."

## THE THERAPEUTIC AND WORKING ALLIANCES

The term alliance refers to the basic partnership that must exist between therapist and patient if the work is to progress. Although the terms have been used in a variety of ways in the literature (Greenson 1967, Zetzel 1965), I prefer to make a distinction between the two terms. I think of the therapeutic alliance in terms of the patient's feelings of trust and safety in the treatment situation. If the therapeutic alliance is not in good repair, the work cannot proceed. If this alliance is lost, the first task is to restore it, whether by interpretation or by management of the crisis that aborted it.

However, more is required for progress than feelings of trust and safety. The working alliance refers to the patient's joining the therapist in working toward the goals of treatment. It is here that the term partnership is most applicable. The working alliance requires access to the observing ego, the patient's capacity to stand back with the therapist in an effort to understand himself both as an individual and in the interpersonal context of the moment.

Attention to the status of the alliances is the task of the therapist. Restoring them when they have been lost is also the task of the therapist. This may require any of the functions described earlier in this chapter. This restoration often offers the opportunity for understanding important interpersonal dynamics and for their interpretation.

# CHAPTER 15

# The Use of Psychotropic Drugs as an Adjunct to Therapy

The therapist may, at times, wonder if including the use of psychotropic drugs as an adjunct to psychotherapy is indicated. There are certainly times when the individual's level of functioning is so compromised that he or she is not able to make use of the psychotherapy or to continue to work or meet responsibilities. At such times, the nonmedical therapist would probably ask for a consultation with a psychiatrist who is familiar with the action of the various drugs and who will monitor the patient from a medical standpoint. A good working relationship is important lest divisive dynamics be set in motion between the two professionals.

There are, however, times when the recommendation for drug treatment has a negative effect on the treatment relationship. Often, in retrospect, we can see that these were times when the recommendation came out of a countertransference anxiety or pressure to perform rather than from a valid clinical indication. A wish to rescue the patient from pain, or the therapist's inability to contain the patient's anxiety or despair, will also lead the therapist to lose faith in psychotherapy at that moment. The following are some examples of such cases.

> In one situation, the patient's frantic histrionic display created anxiety in the therapist lest the young woman do something self-destructive. After the referral to a medical consultant, the patient was angry, concluding that the therapist did not want her to express her feelings, or that the therapist just wasn't strong enough to deal with them. Later in treatment, when these same frantic outbursts would occur, the therapist was able to contain the intensity of affect and to work with what was going on psychologically.
>
> In another situation, the individual was in despair over the deadness that was the result of his distancing and dissociative defenses, defenses that he had quite consciously erected as a boy in the face of his mother's maniacal, eroticized, drunken rages. Referred to a medical consultant, he became angry that the medication led to a numbness of the penis, which was quite likely a conversion reaction that provided a new wall of defense even as the medication threatened to weaken the existing defenses. He was not ready to relinquish these defenses, and in his mind the medication threatened to overthrow them. When the defenses were gradually peeled away with the analytic work

and as he began to remember and to abreact, the question of medication became moot.

An example of the positive effect of medication was one in which the individual was rendered ineffective in her daily work because of the "noise" of an internal, chaotic, assaultive world. The medication effectively stilled the noise and not only enabled her to function at her optimum level at work but also in therapy enabled the strengthening of what Kohut (1977) refers to as compensatory structures,[1] a treatment approach that does not attempt repair of the primary structures because of the severity of their pathology. There was also a softening of her demeanor, a mobilization of her wish to play, and a clear, warmly positive attachment to the therapist. As it also became clear that she was alexithymic, unable to identify and label affect that she only felt in terms of bodily tensions and discomforts, the repair of this deficit was undertaken.

*Alexithymia* (Nemiah 1978) is a term for the failure to make the developmental shift from global psychophysiological distress that normally evolves into specific and differentiated affects that can be described by individuals in their own terms. This development requires the ability of the caretaker to distinguish, correctly label, and appropriately respond to the child's emotional states. The importance of cognitive aspects of the work cannot be overemphasized nonetheless. The establishment of compensatory structures, building new structures that do not eradicate the old but begin to supersede them, is heavily dependent on cognitive components of the work. The emergence of the softer, warmer attachment to the therapist spoke to some early

[1]Kohut calls a structure "defensive" when its sole purpose or predominant function is to cover over the primary defect in the self. He calls a structure "compensatory" when, rather than covering a defect in the self, it compensates for this defect (1977, pp. 4–5).

positive experiences in the preverbal period of her life and would enable the repair of the alexithymia. The potential for intimate and genuine relating was enhanced as well.

In one situation, referral for drugs was interpreted as a transference–countertransference message. In the second situation, medication prematurely endangered the defenses. And in the third situation, the drug seemed to enable repressive defenses to function, protecting the patient from the intrusion of chaotic primitive material. This material could be talked *about* without the patient having to go into it, which would have been so disorganizing as to not be usable for the treatment process. The metaphor of mother's forced feeding stood for the noise content and the patient was able to recognize situations that were analogous to the forced feeding experience and to protect herself from them.

All of this goes to say that the *meaning* of the prescription of medication as well as the effect of the medication—positive or negative—must all be considered. For example, the change in self-feeling engendered by the medication may feel threatening to an individual whose sense of constancy and ongoingness of the self are already fragile. Is there a valid clinical indication for the drug? Is there a countertransference anxiety that motivates the recommendation? When there are two therapists involved, a thorough discussion of the clinical problem will help determine the pros and cons of drug treatment. The psychiatrist's respect for the clinical judgment of the referring therapist is as necessary as the therapist's trust in the judgment of the psychiatrist. When the psychiatrist *is* the primary therapist, it may be too easy to write a prescription, and the clinical decision should include monitoring of the countertransference as well as concern for the effect on the patient's psychological capacity to experience the effect of the medication positively.

# Part IV

---

# The Treatment Process

The treatment process can be divided into specific phases. The shift from one phase to another is likely to be gradual, with a certain amount of overlap. Certain issues will recur through the phases but from differing perspectives. Yet, it is important to consider the specific characteristics of each phase, insofar as each phase will be highlighted by its own concerns and problems. For example, at the beginning, the establishment of trust and of both a therapeutic and working alliance is a primary task. The termination phase will confront the patient (and the therapist) with feelings and tasks associated with separation and loss. Although separation and loss may have been a focus in the earlier phases from the developmental, structural, and dynamic perspective, it now becomes real in the here and now.

The phases of the treatment process can be roughly divided into (1) the opening phase, (2) uncovering, (3) working through, and (4) termination.

Boesky (1990) describes the process in terms of the changes that are to be expected over time. To paraphrase them, they are (1) a gradual and progressive revealing of historical material relevant to the presenting symptoms and a convincing demonstration of the link between them; (2) unfolding in the transference of this historic material and a demonstration of the link between them and how it operates in treatment as a resistance; (3) cooperative interest in understanding the symptoms, associations, dreams, and behavior; (4) relatively enduring change for the better in symptoms and functioning; (5) change in the relationship with the therapist characterized by less disguised behavior and ultimately by more realistic patterns of perception, attitude, and behavior; (6) appearance of dynamically relevant new material; (7) appearance of regressive symptoms, less disguised behavior, and to-and-fro shifts in "progressive" and "regressive" phenomena; (8) shifts in images of the self, of family members, and of the therapist; (9) changes in predominant thematic content; (10) increased tolerance for the expression of sexual and aggressive derivatives, together with increased coherence and clarity of the associations, behavior, dreams, and communications of the patient; (11) increased resistance to regression under stress; (12) improved capacity to cope with unpleasant affects; (13) diminished need for self-punishment (a more mature superego); and (14) increased capacity for realistic gratification.

Although Boesky acknowledges that this is not a definitive catalogue, it is useful to think of the process in these operational terms and to look at them from time to time as a measure of progress or its absence.

# CHAPTER 16

# The Opening Phase

Freud (1933b) retells a story of Victor Hugo's about a Scottish king's claim of having an infallible method of recognizing a witch. He had the woman stewed in a cauldron of boiling water and then tasted the broth. Afterwards he was able to say, "That was a witch," or, "No, that was not one." Freud says it is the same for us, except that *we* are the sufferers. "We cannot judge the patient who comes for treatment . . . till we have studied him analytically for a few weeks or months. We are," he says, "buying a pig in a poke" (p. 155). We should add to this, "and so is the patient."

## BEFORE WE MEET

Schubart (1989) tells us that "facets of transference and countertransference may already find expression in the first psychoanalytic consultation by virtue of the fact that the patient is offered space for the unfolding of his internal situation" (p. 423). But the opening phase of the opening phase seems to go back beyond that hour.

It seems to me that the first meeting between patient and therapist has a great deal in common with the blind date. Both people come into the situation with a variety of wishes and hopes, fears and dreads already in place. From an object relations perspective, these hopes and fears will be consistent with the individual's inner world of self and object and the emotional and dynamic interplay between them.

As noted earlier, these internal representations are themselves derivatives of the individual's earliest interpersonal experience within the context of his or her relationship with the primary caretaking other or others. That is, what was first interpersonal becomes intrapsychic, and what has thus become structured intrapsychically colors or determines subsequent interpersonal experience, or, at least, one's expectations with respect to interpersonal experience. We speak of these predispositions in terms of transference, although they also exist within the therapist. Hopefully, these predispositions will have been addressed in the therapist's own treatment so they will not unduly affect his or her relationship with the patient. That is, countertransference reactions based on the therapist's own unresolved issues will not be brought into the therapeutic relationship.

At the very outset, the situation is at the point of its greatest fluidity—it can go either way; either in the direction of the wish for an emotional connection with a letting down of characteristic defenses, or in the direction of fear of closeness, with an immediate activation of the defenses.

Although the therapist, ideally, does not bring personal needs, wishes, conflicts, or fears into the treatment situation, it is quite likely that he or she *will* hope that the session goes well, that rapport will be established, that a working alliance will be possible, and that the patient will accept the treatment frame with a minimum of protest or resentment. We know there will be a negative transference sooner or later, but we hope it will be readily manageable and responsive to interpretation. Yes, we do write interesting and enlightening papers about the difficult patient, but I doubt if any therapist wishes for such a patient. Furthermore, who does not, at some level, dread the emergence of primitive rage, destructive hate, or paranoid accusation?

The hopes and wishes, dreads and fears that exist before the first meeting are interpersonal in nature. The patient does not enter the consultation room for the first time wishing to have his conflicts resolved or hoping that his developmental deficits will be repaired. He enters the room hoping that the therapist is someone with whom he can feel safe, someone who will like and accept him and who will have the power to help him. He may also enter the room fearing that the therapist will not like him, or dreading that the therapist will say or do something to hurt him, maybe even reject him by refusing to accept him as a patient. Beginning therapists, and maybe even some not that early in their career, are often worried that they will be rejected by a prospective patient. This may come from issues of self-esteem as well as from practice and financial worries. But even the rawest beginner should remember that, by virtue of his or her designated role in the situation as the professional, as the therapist, the significant power that is associated with authority figures will be attributed to him or her by the patient. The patient may feel so endangered by this power that he comes into the situation with self-protective walls firmly in place.

The wishes and fears of the therapist are not unlike those of the patient, for we bring our humanness as well as our professional and clinical expertise, although we may couch them in more appropriately professional terms. Let there be an atmosphere of trust and of a positively charged connection. Let there be an ability to understand the patient and to communicate that understanding, and let there be a positive response to feeling understood. These are not unreasonable hopes or wishes, nor can they be viewed as necessarily indicative of unresolved issues in the therapist. Yet, they constitute the basis for immediate disappointment and for the emergence of countertransference reactions that must be quickly processed if a therapeutic process is even to begin.

This, the opening phase of the opening phase, actually starts before we go out to the waiting room that first time to introduce ourselves and to invite the person into our office. It starts with the referral, when the patient hears about us and we hear about him or her.

## The Referral Process

Our good friend who has arranged the blind date enthusiastically tells us that we and the other person would make a great pair, that we are well suited to one another, that the other person is highly desirable physically, intellectually, and maybe even financially. And that person is probably told something equally enticing about us.

Our colleague who makes the referral tells us this will be an interesting patient, a challenge, rewarding to work with and, yes, he can afford our fee. Meanwhile, the prospective patient is told of our qualifications, of the likelihood that we can help with his or her presenting problem.

Indeed, the source of the referral often introduces anxiety or conflict in the therapist, oftentimes with a sense of performance pressure and anxiety lest the colleague be disappointed in the outcome of the referral. Loss of reputation as well as loss of future referrals looms as the consequences of a failure to perform well.

Sometimes the prospective patient is himself someone prominent or powerful in his own right. This situation can also induce countertransference anxieties that create a pressure to perform, to look good to the patient.

As a therapist who has written professional papers and books, I sometimes find that there is a preexisting transference already in place when the patient is also a therapist and has read that literature. This transference may range from idealization to envy and hate.

All this is to say that before therapist and patient meet, the process is already underway. The first telephone contact also is laden with transference and countertransference potential. The therapist has to be able to keep in mind potential preexisting reactions to the situation that were established well before the first appointment and to be able to process their impact on the beginning treatment process. Whether they are pursued openly with the patient at that time will be a clinical decision. A preexisting idealization of the therapist will be noted, filed away, but not confronted if it is deemed to be a manifestation of a primitive character structure. On the other hand, if there were problems in the mechanics of setting up of the first appointment, these are likely to be embedded in a transference metaphor or in a presenting dream. It will make sense to acknowledge this communication, although any attempt to interpret it beyond that acknowledgment should be held off until there is a clearer understanding of the individual's character structure and the deeper implication of the initial difficulties. This may come fairly soon, for example, when the patient discloses how difficult it felt to get through to her mother. One might say, "It must have felt something like that when you kept getting my answering machine and I didn't call you back right away."

## Values of the Therapist

There may also be philosophical antecedents to how we enter into the therapeutic relationship and the analytic process. Personal values of the therapist may constitute a significant aspect of his or her own identity or ego ideal. These values may be humanistic, pragmatic, or scientific, or a combination of these. They will be part of a built-in interest in helping others, or in problem solving, or in theoretical understanding and theory building. All of these values can certainly be used in the service of defense, as a barrier to the authentic relating of the here and now in the treatment situation. As such, they should be explored in our own therapy. Our basic values, which are an integral aspect of a mature ego ideal, are felt to be *who* we are and affect *how* we are in the world in subtle and unexamined ways. People tend to assume that their basic values have an intrinsic truth, at times forgetting that the values of others may be quite different. Our Western values of self-fulfillment will be at odds with those of a person whose value system embraces sacrifice of self for the group or for God. It would be arrogant of us to assume that those values are indicative of neurosis. The superego, including the ego ideal, will reflect the culture within which the individual developed, although they may at some point become conflicted when self-assertive impulses come to the fore. Can we help them resolve that conflict without attacking their values? That is often a challenge that can only be met if the therapist has an abiding respect for the differentness of others.

When there are fundamental differences in basic philosophies of life that cannot be attributed to neurosis, these differences may generate transference or countertransference phenomena that are analyzable. They may also generate a discomfort that comes from a fundamental failure of fit that will affect the treatment from the start. I'm not sure that reactions on the part of the patient to such a failure of fit can legitimately be viewed as resistance. The making of a match, inside or outside of the treatment situation, will be affected by human factors that are not pathological and that are related to the nature of the fabric of who the person is. In the opening phase of the opening phase there will be a sensing on the part of both participants as to the possibility of fit, and thus of empathy and understanding. The interpersonal wishes and fears that are most active at the first meeting will either be supported or contradicted by these preexisting dispositions in both patient and therapist that are, to a large extent, unconsciously communicated and equally unconsciously perceived.

## Individual Differences

In the service of our illusion of control, whatever our theoretical orientation, be it self psychology, object relations, or classical Freudian, we may fail to acknowledge that there are elements of personality that inevitably color the interpersonal experience and yet that are not pathological, that are neither a manifestation of conflict nor of developmental deficit or structural pathology. These differences may or may not become impediments to smooth relating, and thus may *generate* conflict. It is easier to understand empathically emotions or actions that are in response to interpersonal conflict. It is more difficult to understand empathically and understand certain fundamental differences in how one is human. Perhaps the greatest therapeutic transgression is interpretation of the patient's way of being human as a manifestation of pathology. Unfortunately, this is not all that rare. As an attack on the individual's basic sense of self, because of the power attributed to the therapist, we sometimes work with people with iatrogenically imposed or iatrogenically reinforced damage to the sense of the value of the self or the reality of the self.

The best we can do in the situation of absence of a good fit, is to help both self and patient to deal with it, for coming to terms with differentness from self is a developmental task of the early years. Ultimately, it is our good will and dogged perseverance that may enable treatment to progress despite enormous differences. If this is not possible and the patient has to be referred to someone else, it is most important that he or she not leave with a belief that this is proof of something wrong with him or with her.

We are accustomed to making structural diagnoses in terms of developmental disorders or deficits, or we may try to understand our patient in terms of conflict, anxiety, and defense. We may try to make sense of how the person is with us in terms of his or her early relationships or traumas. Too often we fail to take into account certain healthy, growth-promoting experiences of the mind that may enable the individual not only to compensate for or defend against psychological vulnerabilities, but also to transcend them. The autonomous functions of the ego, the constitutionally endowed capacities to think, to reason, and to create new possibilities, and the opportunities for learning that feed these capacities, come to play as significant a role in the individual's development and are as much a part of who the person is as does the intrapsychic, representational world. Whereas attachment, separation and individuation, and negotiation of the conflicts of the oedipal period are developmental tasks of the earliest years, learning is a major developmental task of the latency years of middle childhood, and the development of a philosophy of life and the setting of goals and values are major developmental tasks of adolescence. Psychoanalysis at times seems strangely unconcerned with these aspects of mind. There is, after all, life beyond Oedipus!

Certainly the achievement of later tasks may be compromised by early developmental failures, as when there was a failure to assimilate the autonomous functions within a core self representation, or when these functions become embroiled in conflict and must be defensively split off or repressed. When these innate capacities have maintained adequate conflict-free status, on the other hand, they not only enable transcendence in the presence of pathology, but they also enrich and elaborate healthy structure and enable the expression of creative potential. We should remember that these constitutionally endowed mental activities are attributes of a core true self, and although they may also serve defensive or compensatory functions, they should never be pathologized or analyzed away. Any interpretation of how they are used to protect the self or to defend against conflict must be made in a way that affirms and acknowledges them as valued and loved aspects of the self.

Although we may turn to the understandings about human nature that have come from the psychoanalytic perspective to guide our work, the very concept of "self" implies a humanistic and existential philosophical underpinning, also guiding us in the therapeutic enterprise.

## THE FIRST SESSION

Since we do not know at the outset what will evoke anxiety or the patient's capacity to bear it, I choose a style that is a combination of open-endedness and structure. If, in allegiance to psychoanalytic technique, the patient is left on his or her own to associate freely, we may inadvertently traumatize the individual. It is my goal, in the first session, to establish an atmosphere of interest in and concern for the individual, as well as to communicate whatever understanding I may come to as to that person's core struggle or concern. This will come from a combination of inquiry and careful listening, attempting to put into words what the individual may not be able to articulate. It is also my goal to provide a sense of safety, to promote the therapeutic alliance, along with an exploration of the person's capacity to join me in the beginnings of a working alliance. At all times, I will try to be sensitive to my impact on the individual as well as to his or her impact on me—that is, to the unfolding transference–countertransference constellation.

When I greet the person in the waiting room and invite him or her to come in, I do so with ordinary social cordiality, neither overly effusive nor overly serious. No matter what we do, it will have an effect, and if this effect is problematic for the patient, we will hear about it in one way or another. We begin allowing everything to wash over us, as it were, screening out nothing, and allowing for our own unconscious synthesizing capacity to perceive metaphor, allusion, threads, and themes.

I will generally indicate where I sit, inviting the individual to sit wherever would be comfortable. The choices are a chair facing mine, or the couch, which also faces my chair. I sit in a swivel rocker that allows me to easily adjust my position to face wherever he or she chooses to sit. I will make note in my mind of how the individual positions himself or herself with respect to me. None of this is commented upon but is part of my getting a feel for the interpersonal atmosphere (of which I am a part, of course).

**The Open-Ended Interview**

Although I have in mind certain avenues of exploration, I proceed in a manner that allows for avenues introduced by the patient, making inquiry when necessary. My manner of inquiry hopefully communicates, "I am interested in you. Tell me more about that. I want to understand you better."

There may be some people who cannot tolerate any degree of control by the therapist, and the inquiry process may feel controlling. If the therapist is empathically in tune with the patient, he or she should be ready to forego any gathering of information through even a modified interview approach. This situation, of course, tells us something about the patient, alerting us to a probable extreme vulnerability of self.

**Presenting Problem**

I will probably begin by asking the person what brings him or her to our meeting. I will want to know something about the duration or circumstances of the problem and how he or she has dealt with it up to then, and if he or she has ever been to a therapist before.

### Previous Therapy

If the individual has had therapy before, I will inquire how it was, if there were any problems that came up in the course of the work, what were some of the main issues that were dealt with, how the therapy ended, and maybe why the person is not returning to his or her previous therapist.

Sometimes we may get caught up in such a way as to mobilize our own arrogance or grandiosity, believing that we will succeed where others have failed. We may be fortunate enough to have that outcome realized, especially if we address transference issues that were not addressed in previous therapies. On the other hand, it is very likely that the problems that emerged with the former therapist will also emerge with us. This piece of history can be very informative as to the nature of the person's interpersonal relationships and the underlying character structure that shapes them.

### The Current Life

Next I will ask the person to tell me something about his or her present life, who is in it, what his or her work or profession is, what day-to-day experience is like. Here again, themes and threads will be expressed, themes and threads that are seen to run consistently through the person's life. A picture of the current level of functioning is important as an indication of areas of ego strength or weakness.

### The History

Next I will ask the person to tell me a little about how it was to grow up – who was in the family, where he or she was in the sibling lineup, and the nature of relationships within the family. I will ask specifically about relationships with the mother, the father, and the siblings.

I will also ask about friendships in childhood and adolescence. The capacity for friendship and peer relating is seriously limited by pathological narcissism. The capacity for friendship and for altruistic concern suggests a more mature level of object relations development.

Psychoanalysts often fail to take into account the impact on the individual's identity and sense of self of a pathological family system in the family of origin. Even a cursory history such as that of this first interview is likely to reveal overtones of such a situation. When the individual is still embroiled in that pathological system, either interpersonally or when internally structuralized, I find that an examination and understanding of the system and the person's role in it is a necessary and integral aspect of the analytic work. The therapist needs to understand the concepts of a systems approach. The concepts of transference and countertransference are systems concepts, albeit a two-person system.

I may also ask what the person's earliest memory is and am struck time and again how the core issue is often embedded within that memory. Sometimes that memory is selected just because it stands as a metaphor for the individual's lifelong struggle.

## Dreams

If I have the sense that the individual is comfortable with a deepening of exploration and is not made too anxious by it, or is not vulnerable to being traumatized to what may be felt as intrusive, I may ask if there are any dreams he or she remembers, recent or old, or even repetitive dreams. Once again, we are likely to find a reaffirmation of what we are able to perceive as an emerging pattern of meaning and concern for the individual.

## Making a Provisional Formulation

If at all possible, as the end of the first hour approaches, I will try to make a provisional formulation of what I perceive as the core struggle. Luborsky and colleagues (1988) found in their research that treatment outcome was dependent on the focus on the core relationship issue, the core interpersonal struggle. This struggle will reflect the character structure, the internal world of self and object and their affective and dynamic interplay, as well as any pathology of the structure itself.

I make this formulation in ordinary language that the person can understand. This is not the place for the language of theory. An example of such a formulation might be, "You seem to be very fearful of saying what you think and feel because you anticipate that the other person will either turn against you or move away from you emotionally. This seems to have happened to you in your growing-up years, and it is an anxiety that you even have here with me today." When this is correct, of course, the person generally feels relieved at being understood, perhaps for the first time. He or she is also relieved at having experiences that have always felt mysterious or irrational and thus, "crazy," articulated in a way that makes these experiences make sense, not only cognitively, but historically. When this happens, the alliance is enhanced, and the individual feels some hope that the therapist may be able to help.

## Monitoring the Transference

I generally will ask, as the end of the hour approaches, how the session has been for him. Transference concerns may be openly expressed at that time. How they will be handled will be a clinical decision. For example, if the person expresses some concerns about trust, I may say that that makes sense, since he doesn't really know me at all, and that we can pay attention to that concern when it comes to the fore. What is communicated is the therapist's readiness to talk about the process in a nondefensive manner and thus the patient's freedom to bring it up.

## Setting the Contract

At this point, I will ask the person how he or she feels about our continuing to meet and what thoughts he or she might have about those meetings. The individual might laugh and say "I'd love to come every day but I can only afford once a week" or with some anxiety might say, "I thought maybe I could come in every other week."

There are two factors to be taken into consideration in the face of this decision; one is reality and financial constraints, and the other will have to do with what is optimal for the prospective patient. As in all clinical decisions—and this is a clinical decision—turning to one's theoretical orientation for a set rule of treatment is often likely to do a disservice to the patient. We need to ask ourselves: Who is this person? How much anxiety is being generated by the process already? How much anxiety can be tolerated? Will more sessions reduce the anxiety or increase it beyond the person's capacity to tolerate it? What arrangement will enhance the process? What arrangement will increase defenses against it? The open-ended question with respect to the individual's ideas about entering into treatment, along with other understanding arrived at over the hour should help the therapist come to an appropriate treatment contract with the individual. Every situation must be approached as unique, and here the therapist's intellectual grasp of the issues, empathic sensitivity to the patient, and willingness to be flexible in order to arrive at the optimal arrangement that will enhance both therapeutic and working alliances will contribute to the final decision.

Once it has been determined that the individual wishes, at least provisionally, to enter into the treatment situation, it is necessary to communicate aspects of the frame that will, one way or another, make certain demands on him. We need to tell him what our fee is if this has not already come up in the session, we need to tell him about the time frame, how long each session will be, and we need to tell him what our cancellation policy is. The latter may cause more difficulty. Some therapists will charge for *all* missed sessions and do not make allowances for vacations taken at a time different from those of the therapist. Others have a policy in which there is no charge if sufficient time is allowed for the therapist to use the open hour productively, such as to offer it to someone else who wants an additional appointment or makeup time, or to schedule a consultation.

## Money Issues in Treatment[1]

It is not likely that we can separate payment for therapy from transference and countertransference input. Freud

[1]Material from this section is taken, in part, from Horner (1991a).

(1913) notes that the transfer of money is an integral part of the treatment with possibly decisive consequences for the course of treatment. Although Kubie (1950) thinks that both therapist and patient should behave as if "money did not exist" (p. 135), it does, in fact, exist, and such behavior is in itself also a stimulus to which the patient may be likely to respond. If anything, the exchange of money is an ongoing reminder about the realities of the relationship and, at times, with certain more impaired individuals, may be the only check on a loss of reality testing and emergence of a psychotic transference. Although some degree of illusion is intrinsic to the treatment setup, the payment of money may be the only factor that prevents illusion from becoming delusion with some patients.

## TRANSFERENCE ISSUES

Confrontation with the inescapable realities of life—death, taxes, and the analyst's bill—will certainly mean different things to different people. When we speak of maintaining the therapeutic frame (see Chapter 8), which must include the exchange of fees, we cannot assume that the frame is inherently neutral. It may be a challenge to the patient's overtly or covertly held illusion of specialness, in which case the need to pay a fee may constitute a narcissistic wound. Narcissistic wounds are never neutral, in spite of the patient's capacity to endure them without overwhelming shame or paranoia. The pragmatic aspects of billing and collecting will be taken in and processed in accordance with the patient's character structure. Preexisting defenses and coping strategies aimed at maintaining narcissistic equilibrium will be brought to bear. Even in those instances in which the payment of the fee is a relief to the patient who characteristically and cynically wonders what interpersonal price will have to be paid in important relationships, unconscious feelings about "having to pay" may still emerge upon each billing or payment in dreams or in transference allusions. These transference reactions will then be available to the work of treatment.

In his discussion of the payment of fees, Eissler (1974) makes it clear that no general statements can be made, that the specific meanings to specific patients will cover a wide spectrum of effects. A wealthy patient who is charged a high fee may see this as further evidence that he is only sought after because of his money, or that if you have anything people will be out to exploit you. In contrast, another wealthy patient may not believe he is getting optimal service unless he pays a corresponding fee.

## COUNTERTRANSFERENCE ISSUES

The therapist's approach to financial arrangements with patients is likely to be multiply determined. Issues such as prevailing peer community standards will enter in as well as the therapist's issues of competition, envy, or masochistic self-denial with respect to his or her peers. The therapist may gain superego gratification by not being as "greedy" as those peers. The therapist's relation to money and what meaning it holds symbolically and dynamically will also be a factor. One's professional ego ideal, one's social values, will play a role. Countertransference issues may be indistinguishable from social values, and they may both be active within a single clinical situation.

For example, a therapist holds values related to helping certain individuals who would be denied treatment unless they were assigned a greatly reduced fee. It is not unlikely that a judgment as to the worthwhileness of the patient will enter into a decision to make such an offer. Already the dynamics are complicated. Having made this offer, our hypothetical therapist may feel good about himself insofar as he is living up to his values. He may be taken aback when a patient reports feeling humiliated by the offer, or burdened by it, feeling the necessity to make up the financial sacrifice by making the therapist's work pleasant or easy. He will have to be a rewarding patient one way or another. The patient may also be suspicious of the analyst's motives and wonder what will be asked in return. Instead of trust being generated, it is shaken. Our hypothetical therapist may feel wounded, his altruism having been misunderstood or unappreciated. Countertransference may now be in full swing.

This all goes to say that practical, day-to-day decisions with respect to money matters in the therapeutic relationship are never simple matters of policy. Yet, policy decisions are required on a regular basis in one's practice. Assuming that the therapist is, for the most part, aware of his own dynamics with respect to money, I would like to suggest a principle that will guide clinical decisions entailing the payment or nonpayment of fees. This principle, simply stated, is that one's policy decisions should not traumatize the patient, that the therapist adhere as closely as possible to a stance of clinical neutrality in making these decisions. For an elaboration of what constitutes clinical neutrality, the reader is referred back to Chapter 7. In sum, neutrality embodies the goal of establishing an optimal tension between the patient's tendency to see the therapist as an old object (i.e., transference), and the capacity to experience the therapist as a new and essentially benign and self-enhancing object.

The closer our decisions with respect to money matters in treatment can come to being true clinical decisions based on our understanding of the patient's character structure and dynamics, the less likely we are to act out our countertransference motives even when countertransference issues are operating.

There are many situations that come up around the payment of fees, such as payment for missed sessions, third-party payment, raising fees, reducing fees, or allowing a bill to accumulate. Taking the maintenance of therapeutic neutrality as a guiding principle, one cannot make across-the-board statements about any of these. When we try to do so, we inevitably get caught up in our own beliefs, values, needs, and rationalizations of them or in theoretically narrow concepts that inevitably do a disservice to one patient or another. Other elements that may not seem as prone to evoking transference reactions may well do so, such as the conduct of the business end of one's practice by a secretary, or the mailing of bills and checks with no hand-to-hand exchange of money taking place. There may be an unconscious collusion between therapist and patient that constitutes the denial of money as an issue. Sooner or later something is likely to emerge that will reveal this collusion. It will be up to the therapist to perceive this information and to work with it.

# CHAPTER 17

# The Process Continues

## NATURE OF THE PROCESS

As we set out to describe the process of psychoanalytic therapy, it is useful to keep in mind what Freud (1913) came to realize relatively early in his work.

> The analyst . . . cannot determine beforehand exactly what results he will effect. He sets in motion a process, that of the resolving of the existing repressions. He can supervise this process, remove obstacles

in its way, and he can undoubtedly vitiate much of it. But on the whole, once begun, it goes its own way and does not allow either the direction it takes or the order in which it picks up its points to be prescribed for it. [p. 130]

Abend (1990) notes that this observation is as cogent today as it was in 1913. He writes:

> We must still admit that no matter how confident the analyst may be in his or her understanding of the patient, and in the application of his or her technique, much of what transpires in analysis is beyond the analyst's ability to predict, influence, or explain. [p. 546]

This observation confronts the therapist with his or her own limits and requires from the therapist an ability to tolerate ambiguity, uncertainty, and unpredictability. Hopefully, it will also reassure the beginning therapist that this aspect of the process does not indicate some personal failing.

However, Abend, who comes from a classical analytic position, is not taking a nihilistic stance with respect to the role the analyst plays in the treatment situation. He adds:

> This is not to suggest that . . . what goes on within the patient, once set in motion by the impact of analysis, thereafter proceeds independently of the analyst's further interventions . . . we would probably all agree that the analyst's attitudes, thinking, and activities all continuously affect the patient throughout the duration of the analysis. Furthermore . . . [the patient's] attitudes, thinking, and activities also exert a continuous influence on the analyst. These mutual influences contribute to the formation of an extraordinarily intricate network of constantly shifting inter-

> actions, of which only a certain portion are ever fully identified and understood, even in the most successful analyses. [p. 547]

Arlow and Brenner (1990) also emphasize that the process does not unfold in a simple linear fashion. "There are advances and retreats, progression and regression, diversions and distortions, all along the way" (p. 680). They tell us that the process *will not* evolve on its own, will not take place automatically. It requires the application of the therapist's understanding and interventions. A totally passive stance on the part of the therapist does not automatically set the stage for the full unfolding of the patient.

## STAGES OF THE PROCESS

Langs (1974) defines the opening phase of treatment as

> that period of treatment, however long (and it may range from a week to many months), during which the patient's emotional problems and need for treatment are being defined, and a firm and positive therapeutic alliance is being established. This phase continues as long as there are major doubts about the patient's motives for seeking treatment and willingness to explore his problems, and about the establishment of a lasting alliance. [p. 379]

Despite a certain amount of overlap of the phases of treatment, we become aware of shifts in the nature of the therapeutic relationship and in the capacity to relinquish defenses and confront the basic issues. Langs describes the middle phase of treatment as follows:

> I would define the middle phase of treatment as the period that extends from the establishment of a firm or at least a workable therapeutic alliance to the serious introduction of termination. It is the main phase devoted to exploring, analyzing, working through and resolving the patient's symptoms, and emotional and characterological problems. It is the heart of treatment. . . . [p. 423]

Although the word *termination* suggests an event, termination in analytic psychotherapy is a phase, sometimes relatively short, and sometimes constituting a significant segment of the overall process.

There are times when treatment is discontinued before a termination phase can evolve organically, as it does under optimal circumstances.

There are forced terminations, as when the therapist leaves the clinic where he is seeing the patient, or when the therapist or patient moves. There are forced terminations due to illness, loss of a job, or an inability to afford treatment.

There are interruptions of treatment that are actually part of the process and can usefully be understood and supported as such.

## THE PHASES OF TREATMENT

### Uncovering

I prefer to divide the opening phase into the first session and what goes before it, and the phase of *uncovering,* in which the basic issues of either conflict or structural impairment unfold before us in the content of the sessions, in the memories and associations that are evoked within the session, and in the transference–countertransference experience. It is in the earlier phase of the overall process that transference and countertransference will be most intense and through which the uncovering will take place.

The various resistances—the defenses that are manifest in the therapeutic situation—will be called into play from the start. It is the gradual understanding of these defenses and the dangers behind them, the dangers that the individual must protect himself or herself from, that will enable the individual to relinquish them sufficiently to allow for a deeper level of exploration. This will necessitate a relative resolution of the major transference issues that also preclude this deeper exploration.

An essential aspect of the uncovering phase and its above desiderata will be the firming up of both therapeutic and working alliances, along with a reliably available observing ego. The uncovering phase is likely to be the stormiest phase and the time during which a flight from treatment or a malignant disruption of the treatment is likely to occur. This phase may be relatively short, but it may also be quite long and the individual may seem to fall back into the same issues from time to time even as there seems to have been a movement forward to the next phase, that of *working through*. Nevertheless, these regressions should be relatively brief and amenable to interpretation.

## Working Through

The working-through phase finds the individual remembering more of his or her early experiences, filling in the gaps and spaces and making increasingly understandable the evolution of the self both in terms of health and strength as well as in terms of conflicts, deficits, or problems in the world. The individual's unique makeup, uncluttered by pathology and its consequences, also comes more to the fore, and this is a time of exquisite sensitivity to the therapist's response to that unique self.

Whatever the person's early developmental history, it began with a unique organism with certain inborn features that include basic temperament (Chess and Thomas 1977) as well as aspects of brain function that determine the very working of the mind, whether the individual is inclined more to a cognitive style dominated by logic and reason, or a mind style that includes to a great degree intuitive perception of pattern and paradox and symbolic thinking. The latter style may lead the individual to a more inward focus, a more solitary approach to thinking and learning. It is damaging when this is pathologized, perhaps labeled evidence of a schizoid personality. Yet, such people are often very capable of mature intimacy and affective relating.

During the working-through phase the distinction between defensive structures or strategies and the unique personhood should become clear and should be acknowledged. It is usually difficult for the patient to perceive his or her own health when it has been obscured by a pathological overlay.

During the working-through phase there will be a diminished transference focus and an increasing back and forth between present-day experience in the world and its historical and characterological antecedents. The individual will increasingly be able to see those connections, to separate past and memory from the here and now, and to divest himself or herself from a belief system that was set up in childhood within the context of that child's experience. In therapy, the child's experience is brought to consciousness where the adult is able to reconsider it with all of the intellect, experience, sophistication, and cognitive maturity that life has brought.

The working-through process has a strong cognitive element in this respect, and interferences with cognitive functioning itself have to be dealt with before this is possible. Such interferences may be, for example, concrete thinking, syllogistic thinking, or categorical thinking and overgeneralization. These often must be addressed directly in the uncovering phase as part of a defensive style.

Transference issues do not disappear, yet when they do come forward once again, individuals are more likely to realize the origins of these reactions. They are more likely to say, "I don't know why I have this feeling. I certainly *know* that you aren't like that at all." Or they may report a dream that can be seen to have both transference and developmental levels of understanding. Again, they may be puzzled as to why they should have any such residual transference phenomena. Assuming that the individual is not correctly responding to something the therapist actually said or did, but rather to a feared reaction or to attributed meaning, it may help to reassure the individual by pointing out that the unconscious still makes those connections despite what he or she has consciously come to realize in the course of treatment.

During the working-through process there should be a resolution of conflict and/or a repair of structural deficit that will enable the individual to move into the last phase of treatment, winding down the process and confronting the issues of ending per se. Table 17-1 illustrates the phases of treatment and the resolution aspect of the working-through phase in the case of the oedipal patient.

**Table 17-1. Steps Necessary to Resolve the Oedipus Complex**

| Steps | Opposite-sex parent | Same-sex parent |
|---|---|---|
| 1. Uncovering | | |
| Acknowledge wish, fantasy, or desire | To have sexually and/or to be the preferred object | To defeat in competition and to displace; to murder |
| Understand fear associated with the wish | Loss of control | Punishment (e.g., castration or withdrawal of love); guilt |
| Understand negative affect associated with frustration | Anger; feelings of betrayal; sense of failure or inadequacy; sadness, yearning | Humiliation; envy |
| 2. Working through | | |
| Insight into how conflicts are played out (a) in present day life (b) in the transference | Interference with heterosexual relationships | Interference with achievement of goals and ambitions |
| 3. Resolution | | |
| Renunciation of the wish | To have sexually and/or to be the preferred object | To defeat in competition and to displace |
| Acceptance of parents as real people | Without the need to idealize or disparage | Without the need to idealize or disparage |
| Acknowledgment of identifications | With opposite-sex parent without endangerment of gender identity and/or the ego ideal | With same-sex parent without endangerment of the ego-ideal |
| Neutralization of drive | Desexualization of affection toward parent of opposite sex | De-aggressivization of strivings for success and achievement |
| Redirection of strivings | To new love object. Reunion of sex and affection without guilt or anxiety | Toward ambitions. Strivings for success and achievement without guilt or anxiety |
| 4. Termination | | |
| Therapist is perceived in realistic terms as adult equal | Patient withdraws emotional investment in treatment and redirects it toward his real life | Patient actively takes over full responsibility for own life |

From *Treating the Oedipal Patient in Brief Psychotherapy,* ed. A. Horner. New York: Jason Aronson, 1985.

## Termination

Dewald (1982) tells us:

> It is difficult to overestimate the importance of the termination phase in the treatment process, or the impact difficulties in this phase may have on the final resolution and outcome on treatment, be it in psychoanalysis or in psychotherapy. [p. 441]

And he later adds:

> . . . the patient must begin to experience, work through, and resolve the various reactions that separation from and loss of the relationship to the analyst stimulate. [p. 442]

In a mini-recapitulation of the phases themselves, more is uncovered and has to be worked through within the termination phase. These issues will again bring to the fore the transference as well as countertransference and the therapist's feelings and attitudes toward termination.

Dewald refers to the therapist's "Pygmalion fantasy" (p. 448), to the therapist's investment in his or her own concept of a perfect outcome, with the patient the perfect product of his or her work. Sometimes this is rationalized in theoretical terms. Any resistance the therapist has to ending treatment, whatever its origin, may lead to a collusion with the patient's resistances, or even worse, may evoke iatrogenic guilt in the patient for his own impetus to bring treatment to a close.

Rose (1974) writes about another kind of inability to terminate.

> There are analyses which, however long they proceed, continue to produce interpretable material while termination

> seems forever unattainable. Either the goal remains distant though progress continues or the termination phase appears always to be just ahead. There is abundant evidence that more analysis is needed and that complete analysis is possible. As faith in the process is renewed by hard-won insights, the work of analysis goes on accurately, if interminably, by mutual consent. Analysis becomes the focus of satisfactions and frustrations, the activity which, above most others, gives meaning and direction to life. Much the same may be said of some therapists; therapist and analysand become married to analysis, if not to each other. [p. 509]

And, he adds later, treatment "is a precious and unique instrument for living and not its replacement. Its value lies in opening up possibilities and not in reducing life to its own instrumentality" (p. 515).

Freud (1937) went right to the point saying:

> Our aim will not be to rub off every peculiarity of human nature for the sake of a schematic "normality," nor yet to demand that the person who has been "thoroughly analysed" shall feel no passions and develop no internal conflicts. The business of analysis is to secure the best possible psychological conditions for the functions of the ego; with that it has discharged its task. [p. 250]

In Chapter 18 we will consider new approaches of brief therapy that take Freud's dictum to heart.

Modell (1991) comments on the genuine bond that develops between therapist and patient, how patients may feel genuine love for their therapists and therapists for their patients. But, he reminds us, "Unlike other love relations . . . the partners will inevitably separate when the aim of treatment has been realized; this separation is a fact that neither participant can forget" (p. 13).

With the issue of the importance of the termination phase thus addressed, what may we expect when this phase proper comes to the fore?

The patient's issues will be directly related to the core issues and conflicts insofar as the therapist has played a role in their resolution or insofar as resolution of a transference is required for termination to be possible.

If the therapist has facilitated structural repair as described in Chapter 5, the patient may be anxious that change will not be sustainable without the therapist. Loss will thus be associated with the early anxieties, as when early object loss for whatever reason traumatized the child. Nevertheless, a reworking through of these issues and their complexities should make it possible for the patient to tolerate the anxiety. The therapist's support of the patient's growth facilitates the working through of reexperienced rapprochement issues insofar as individuation is supported rather than punished. The good-enough therapist can be internalized and be carried with the individual later on as a new internal good object.

Not too long ago I received a call from a woman I had last seen nine years previously. She had wanted to end at that time to see if she could make it on her own. She told me on the telephone that she had finally finished her work with me, work that had continued intrapsychically in spite of the fact that we had not met during those years. It is *crucial* that that kind of termination, that is, with work still to be done, *not* be interpreted as a resistance. To do so would once again give the individual the message that there is something wrong with wanting to individuate and be independent, or that the therapist has no confidence in the patient's gains.

An example of the apparent return of early issues is observed with individuals who have used detachment as a defense against the shame and/or vulnerability of needing and the pain of wanting what cannot be had. They are sometimes likely to resurrect this defense in the face of impending termination. It is likely that they will not bring their feelings about termination up directly. The therapist must either be able to hear the metaphors embedded in the context of the hours or must take the initiative in confronting the reemerged defensive detachment. This is critical lest the individual experience a post-therapy depression. An integral aspect of character change in this instance is the opportunity to internalize the new good object. It is important to help the patient understand the distinction between separation and loss. Separation is an external event. Loss is an internal experience resulting from disconnection from the object, leading, in effect, to object loss. It is this kind of loss that leads to a depressive reaction. The ability to tolerate the sadness of separation and the experience of missing is part of the process of staying connected even though people are no longer together. These issues most surely would have been dealt with in the uncovering and working-through phases of treatment. But they reemerge when it is the therapy relationship that is coming to a close.

*Variations of Termination*

The *organic* termination is one that evolves out of the process. The shift to this phase is generally observed by both therapist and patient. As often as not, it will be the patient who comments upon the shift.

The *forced* termination comes about because of circumstances external to the treatment process or to the therapy relationship. It is necessitated in some instances by the completion of a training assignment for the therapist. He or she leaves the clinical setting to go elsewhere. In the section on brief therapy, I will comment on the value of using a brief therapy format in such settings to reduce these endings that are often traumatic for the patient when a supposedly long-term treatment has been undertaken. Negative consequences include a reluctance to attach to another therapist, a hostility to the new therapist that makes the development of a therapeutic alliance impossible, or a retreat from the treatment process altogether. In some training settings, we observe the development of an institutional transference, in which the patient becomes attached to the hospital or building in which the treatment takes place. This allows for an easy negotiation of sequential changes of therapists. However, it also makes unlikely the establishment of the kind of human connection within which change can take place.

*Traumatic* terminations are those in which the treatment is cut off because of a severe deterioration or disruption of the therapeutic alliance. This may be an angry acting out on the part of the patient, perhaps an "I'll leave you before you can leave me." Even if the alliance cannot be repaired, it is well to have at least one session in which there can be a clarification of what happened in a manner that will make it possible for the individual to resume treatment with someone else if not with the same therapist. This may be a difficult meeting for the therapist who must be able to explore what happened in a nondefensive manner.

A *developmental* termination in one that makes sense dynamically, although the repair and growth process is by no means complete. This is likely to occur with the individual who is working through rapprochement issues in the transference. There is an “I want to try it on my own” message. Just as it is critical that the parent support the small child at this phase as well as the moving away of the adolescent son or daughter, it is important that the therapist also be supportive of the move. It must be clear that the door is always open but also that the therapist has confidence in the patient’s capacity for greater independence at this time. Some therapists will interpret the wish to discontinue treatment as an acting out against the transference, which may be as undermining as the parent who punishes the move by withdrawal of love or who undermines it by a vote of no confidence. When this step is handled well, the patient is likely to return in the future with gains consolidated and with a wish to deal with new issues that emerge at the higher level of ego organization.

*Steps of the Organic Termination*

Once there is a recognition that it is appropriate to begin to think about termination, it is useful to think about a date as well. I find that the patient generally has a pretty good sense of the amount of time that is required to work through the feelings and conflicts associated with this task. Generally, the deeper the overall process has gone with respect to the individual’s self-exploration, and the earlier the developmental issues that have been joined, the longer the termination process will be. The less regression that has occurred overall, the shorter this process. In brief therapy, where regression is avoided through constant interpretation of the transference, termination may be brought up and effected all in one session.

The setting of the date makes the ending real. There is no “Someday we won’t be meeting any more.” This is not a process that is likely to actually take place in life outside the treatment setting. What can be worked through are all the endings and losses that are intrinsic to life: the loss of the mother and father of childhood, the loss of the family as a place of refuge or retreat, the loss of powerful figures who have the power to make things right—in general the loss of many of the illusions of childhood and youth, that life goes on forever, that no one dies, that the self stays young forever, and that, if you are good, all your wishes will come true. The ability to tolerate the feelings associated with loss without defensive maneuvers that prevent its working through, an ability that has been achieved as the result of therapy, enables the termination to take place with a desired internalization of the therapy relationship much as the good-enough mother is internalized to become part of the self in early development. With the mitigation of narcissistic entitlement, the capacity for gratitude has emerged. With the renunciation of idealizing illusions, genuine love can be experienced and kept as memory.

Although old issues may reemerge, the individual will be able to handle and resolve them on his own with what he has learned in therapy. The presenting problem is adequately resolved, and the goals of therapy relatively attained. There is a more realistic and integrated perception of the individual's past and the people in it, as well as a more realistic and integrated perception of himself. Whatever life may have in store, the good termination finds the individual ready to live that life authentically and fully.

## Post-Therapy Relationships

There is some controversy as to the clinical and/or ethical propriety of a relationship between the therapist and a former patient. There is little disagreement that ending treatment *for the purpose of* having a personal relationship is an acting out of the transference–countertransference situation. The patient is deprived of a working through of the transference and of a termination phase and all that it entails. The patient also loses a therapist in the process and no longer has that kind of special relationship and what it enables and provides. And it is very likely that, in some way, the therapist will be exploiting the transference for his or her own needs or gratification. This is particularly true if the post-therapy setup entails a sexual involvement as well. State laws and professional ethics committees have made the impropriety of this situation clear.

There is also what is considered a gray area, of a post-therapy relationship being established at some considerably later time, such as several years after termination. Still, the transference can never be completely resolved insofar as the image the patient has of the former therapist is still likely to be of someone who is so interested in him or in her that all personal wishes and feelings are put aside. Even though unrealistic idealizations of the therapist have been resolved, there is very likely to be an idealization of the structure of the relationship, which is sure to set the ex-patient up for serious disappointment, anger, or feelings of betrayal, with no possibility of working these feelings through.

It is quite likely that there are some exceptions to this probability. Nevertheless, it is the feeling of the majority that some element of exploitation of the transference is inevitable. As therapists, our ethical responsibility to our patients continues even after the work is done, and a great deal of soul-searching should be done if a therapist is confronted with such a situation. It is also the feeling of many that "once the therapist, always the therapist," meaning that the individual always has the option of returning for more work to the one person who probably knows him or her better than anyone else in the world. A personal relationship removes this option.

Less clear are those situations in which the patient becomes a professional colleague. However, this is an eventuality that is likely to be known during the treatment itself, and dealing with the feelings about later probable encounters should be part of the work of termination. In this way, transference aspects can be anticipated and worked through.

Whatever the post-therapy situation, it is incumbent on the therapist to understand its impact on the patient and to act in the best interest of the patient.

# CHAPTER 18

# Brief Psychotherapy

Brief psychoanalytic therapy comes closer to classical psychoanalysis insofar as it is based on the model of a neurotic character (developed beyond the preoedipal stages of development) in which the focus is on the analysis of unconscious conflict, anxiety, and defense with strict attention to the interpretation of the transference. It is not intended for the treatment of more severe personality and character disorders, although there are circumstances in which the technique can be adapted for that population. This situation will be discussed later in this chapter.

Inasmuch as this book has been designed for the less experienced or beginning therapist, it is important to emphasize that brief psychotherapy is not easier to do. Quite the contrary: it requires the ability to make quick determinations as to character structure and the appropriateness of this form of treatment for the individual, in the first session in fact, and it requires the therapist to be sufficiently in control of the treatment to adhere to the brief format and its goals. As such, doing brief treatment may be experienced as in opposition to the precepts of treatment put forth in this book. However, a careful selection of patients ensures that the individual's character structure will not be unduly stressed by this more active and confrontative approach, even though it evokes high levels of anxiety in the patient. There is a reliable working alliance, and the patient is highly motivated to do the work. In this selection process, we want to see if the individual (1) has the ability to form meaningful give-and-take (not narcissistically determined) relationships, (2) has the ability to tolerate strong affects associated with anger, guilt, depression, and anxiety, (3) shows characterological flexibility, and (4) demonstrates a positive response to interpretation. The reader is referred back to Chapter 10 and the discussion of character structure and diagnosis.

The reader is also referred to the brief therapy literature (Horner 1985) and to obtaining direct supervision if he or she wants to become competent in this way of working. Some of the general principles will be discussed here.

## PRINCIPLES OF THE TECHNIQUE

Beyond the importance of the selection process, once the treatment is underway the following principles can be enunciated.

1. The therapist plays an active role and does not passively sit back and wait for things to unfold.

2. A focus of the treatment must be defined quickly, this focus being the core conflict, the anxiety it generates, and the defenses erected against that anxiety. The maintenance of the focus is critical lest the treatment veer off into other directions that, although potentially productive, will lead in the direction of a long-term therapy. With the oedipal patient, this focus will be the oedipal conflict itself. Other approaches to brief treatment may attend to a different focus. For example, Mann (1973b) writes about loss as a focus. The very brevity of the treatment brings loss forward in the transference from the start.

3. Regression is to be prevented through interpretation, through a once-weekly face-to-face format, and through prompt and consistent interpretation of the transference wishes and fears.

4. Interpretations will link the transference, the current relationships, and the historical relationships, demonstrating the dynamic connection among them. This triad of transference–present–past is consistently pointed out. For example, the wish to be special to Father, to be special with the boss, and to be special to the therapist are tied together dynamically. Research in brief therapy outcome has shown that positive results are directly correlated with transference–past connections. It is critical that the transference not be avoided and thus that it be repeatedly dissolved by interpretation.

5. Interpretations will also consistently demonstrate the link between the nature of the conflict, the anxiety, and the defense, another triad. For example, the anxiety and the guilt associated with the conflict between the wish to love and the wish to compete with the parent of the same sex may be defended against with a reaction-formation in which aggression is transformed to placating behavior and turned against the self. The result may be the sabotage of potential success, the presenting problem in some situations.

6. Interpretation of the resistances must also be made quickly and consistently. Although this will evoke a high level of anxiety as will the approach in general, if the patient has been properly selected, he or she will be able to contain this anxiety and work with it. The therapeutic and working alliances will be reliable as will the observing ego.

7. In order to stay within the higher level of ego organization and prevent regression that will lead into preoedipal issues, we interpret upward. That is, although there may be a perseverating preoedipal issue, the interpretation is made in the context of the oedipal triangle. Fear of the loss of Mother's love is interpreted not as a barrier to individuation, but as a barrier to moving toward Father without guilt, anxiety, or depression.

8. Another triad to be addressed is the oedipal triangle when there is an oedipal focus. That is, both mother and father issues must be confronted.

9. We may say with some degree of certainty that when there is an impasse in treatment, long or brief, it is probably due to unanalyzed transference resistances that are being acted out in the treatment situation. We cannot afford to let such an impasse go on in brief therapy for obvious reasons. The therapist's resistance to exploring the patient's resistance should be attended to promptly in supervision. For the therapist in private practice who does not have the supervisory oversight, energetic self-supervision is essential to the success of brief treatment.

## ADAPTATION OF THE TECHNIQUE FOR THE PREOEDIPAL PATIENT

Unfortunately, we are sometimes faced with making a treatment plan based on necessity rather than on its being the treatment of choice. This is especially true when insurance plans place a limit on the number of sessions to be allowed, or on clinic situations in which trainees move on to other placements after six months or a year. What can we do to limit damage done by forced termination and, at the same time, to maximize the benefit the patient might receive? If the patient is being treated with a long-term approach in which the attachment to the therapist plays a significant role in the overall treatment process and is thereby encouraged, the forced termination can only be experienced as a betrayal of trust or an abandonment, thereby leaving the individual with iatrogenic trauma. Future treatment, if the individual even dares to try again, will surely be compromised.

Responding to the ethical concept of informed consent, it makes sense that in such situations the patient know from the start that the treatment will be time limited, that a focus *appropriate to that particular patient* be defined, and that the principles of brief treatment are followed with due consideration for the vulnerabilities of the individual. Transference is examined *within the defined focus*. This focus may be the difficulty the person has in keeping a sense of boundary between himself and others. The focus will consider how this happens in the treatment situation, in present-day relationships, and how it was experienced growing up in the context of the relationships within the family. This dilemma can be explored in all its ramifications, counting on helping the person develop a cognitive handle on the experience along with the healthier defenses that will be enabled by understanding. There will be less push for affect inasmuch as it is likely to have regressive or even disorganizing consequences. The therapist's resistance to a cognitive approach may be a problem in this situation. It is helpful to understand that the self representation is an overarching cognitive structure along with the affect and impulse that it contains.

Kavanagh (1985) reports studies that showed that "some more disturbed patients receiving supporting psychotherapy unexpectedly showed structural change too, becoming better organized with respect to basic ego functions" (p. 560). Since changes in the representational world are in significant part a cognitive achievement, a predominantly cognitive approach to brief psychotherapy of the patient with a structural deficit, with the core developmental issue as the agreed-on focus, might be expected to lead to some degree of enduring structural change.

# Part V

---

# Consultations

In this section, I will present clinical material based on a series of one-time consultations that I had with therapists who were dealing with patients in ongoing therapy. The educational aim of this section is to familiarize the reader with an approach to thinking that endeavors to organize the clinical data in a particular way. This is one in which the treatment process is understood in terms of object relations development and the overall structure of the patient's internal world.

The therapists who consulted me were either unable to formulate the critical issues or felt that the therapy was at an impasse. The exploration of the transference–countertransference situation in particular would generally open the way to an understanding of what aspect of the patient's inner world of self and object representations was manifest in the treatment relationship and how this related to the individual's developmental history of primary relationships as well as to the presenting problem. With this better understanding, the therapists were generally able to move the treatment process forward productively.

# CHAPTER 19

## Rosemary: Transference Resistance

The patient was a 44-year-old woman who had been in treatment with the presenting therapist for 8 months. Although she was of at least average intelligence, she was not articulate and did not express her feelings. Rosemary was a schoolteacher with two children of her own. She was married, and the presenting problem was related to stresses within the marriage. Significant was the source of the referral, a former patient who had been seen briefly by this same therapist in a clinic setting. They had what appeared to be an overly involved, or enmeshed, almost mother–son relationship. From the beginning of the presentation, it was apparent that there was an even wider enmeshed system in which the therapist had been unwittingly involved. The husband's jealousy of his wife's friend had become an issue. Rosemary said she loved her husband but did not want to be with him. Rosemary's daughter was bulimic, and the two of them had a relationship that would also be characterized as enmeshed.

Rosemary described herself as a people pleaser. Of course, this immediately brings to mind the probability that she related to the therapist in a similar manner. It is preferable to address this transference resistance (the patient's attempts to manage and control the therapeutic relationship) as early as possible insofar as little of substance can take place for the patient from this adaptive posture.

In the fifth session, the patient reported that she would make superficial, self-inflicted wounds. She would do this after she had an argument with her husband, when she felt trapped and that there was no way out. If the husband pushed for sex, she would be relieved of her troublesome feelings later by cutting herself. The therapist ascertained that Rosemary was not suicidal. Although we do not immediately have the answer, this would be a time to at least formulate in the mind the question as to the psychological function of hurting herself and to wonder how this related to feeling trapped and to a readiness to become involved in enmeshed relationships. Making hypotheses is part of this consultation process and one could wonder about the patient's need to feel the pain of the self-wounding in order to feel separate and thus more real. It is useful to inquire of the patient what she experiences as she wounds herself. What goes through her mind? The answer may address the motive quite directly. She might say something like, "If I feel the pain I know I exist." Opening the line of inquiry is the responsibility of the therapist.

During the course of treatment the husband left the home, although he came home to do his laundry. Rosemary did not want him there, yet afterwards, she would feel very alone. In this is evident the intensely conflictual nature of her relationships in which both an intense need to have as well as to be rid of the other could be seen. This makes one think of the daughter's bulimia, that is, the daughter's inner world reflected the intense ambivalence of the mother.

At first, Rosemary described hers as an ideal childhood, with a mother who was all good and a father who, although seen in less glowing terms, was not seen negatively. The mother was reported as being always available and gave the child what she wanted. Mother was also described as reserved, however, and Rosemary recalled that she often seemed not to look at her. Father was then revealed as alcoholic, as having outbursts, berating her about her weight.

At the present time, both parents were dead. When the mother was dying of cancer, Rosemary took care of her and would get in bed with the mother and hold her.

It was at this point in the presentation that I inquired about the transference–countertransference situation. The therapist reported feeling like a nonperson and feeling frustrated. It appeared that she had not explored the transference, that she did not bring the issue of people pleasing forth as it took place in the treatment itself.

It also became evident that the therapist had become involved in a system that involved both her former and present patients, as well as the husband. The husband and the friend would call the therapist and report their concern about Rosemary. This pattern of calling one person in the system about another person in the system was well established. It was clear that the boundaries of the treatment frame were as undefined as the patient's self–other boundaries, marital boundaries, or generational boundaries. The treatment and the therapist had been co-opted into the existing system, which could account for the therapist's experience of self as a nonperson and as frustrated in any attempt to function as a therapist. From a consultation perspective, this issue would have to be confronted and the systems dynamics explored, and a safe frame between the therapeutic dyad would have to be maintained. Within that context, the therapy relationship could be explored in terms of the transference resistance, the pleasing of the therapist, along with the anxieties that lay behind this behavior. The fear of object loss if she did not become the other's selfobject was countered by the existential annihilation of doing so. It was this dilemma that would become the core issue of the treatment. The discovery of the hidden true self would be part of this process, and in this aspect the therapist's capacity to be the patient's selfobject would be important, as one who would help her perceive and integrate the intrinsic aspects of her self. But first, the dynamics of the system as well as the false-self defense would have to be interpreted.

# CHAPTER 20

# Isobel: Eroticizing of Power

This patient was a 45-year-old woman. There had been sixteen sessions at the time of this presentation. Isobel had been married several times, always to rich and powerful men. She had three children. She complained of chronic fatigue, was hypochondriacal, and described herself as a health nut. She drank and used drugs from time to time, went to many doctors, and participated in various retreats, always looking for answers outside herself. She had some minor success in the art field.

Isobel came from a poor southern background. There was no father in the home in her early years. She lived with her mother until she was 3, and was left with her grandmother off and on from 3 to 7. The grandmother was reported as stable and as a relatively positive figure. Isobel returned to live with her mother at the age of 7 when the mother remarried. This man was described as mean and controlling. Isobel was afraid of him and was a good girl. When she was 9, her mother divorced again and she returned to live with her grandmother until the age of 11. She came back to live with her mother at this time and with a new stepfather who, although he traveled a great deal and drank, was nice to her. She formed an attachment to him and still has contact with him.

Mother died when Isobel was 40. They were very attached. Mother was described as charismatic, bright, lively, but also as depressed and hypochondriacal. She died as a result of substance abuse. From the time Isobel was 9, Mother seemed to fade. She was in bed a lot, and Isobel cooked for her. Mother died in an institution and Isobel feels guilty, saying she killed her mother by abandoning her.

As a young teen, Isobel hung out with the kids of her lower-middle-class group and had fantasies of owning a Thunderbird. It became her goal in life. As the consultation proceeded, we tried to understand the metaphor of the T-bird, an expensive, sleek, and powerful automobile.

At the time, Isobel had just begun to date a man she knew to be alcoholic and a womanizer, as were the previous men in her life.

Sessions tended to start with her behaving in a mean and tough manner. She would be angry, helpless, and agitated. By the end of the hour she would appear much softer. When her behavior was mean, her male therapist would hold himself distant, was quiet, and had no sense of what would happen. As she softened, he would feel warmer toward her, and he felt this to be sustaining for him. That is, he would alternately allow himself to feel close and then would retreat and distance himself in the face of her aggression. Quite likely this was what the patient had experienced in her growing-up years, with a similar moving toward and then away from the primary object.

I inquired where she appeared to be vulnerable, and this focused on her children, on her guilt at not doing the best she could. She was like a teenager with men, cute and flirtatious, playing this out with her therapist as well. Her attitude of entitlement was evident, suggesting the prominence of narcissistic issues. The question of the eroticizing of power, as first manifest in her lust for the powerful automobile in adolescence, and her lust for powerful men as an adult, would need exploration.

Isobel did show affect, crying when upset. She was most deeply upset at her mother's dying. She felt alone and wanted to be with her. She recalled waiting on the front steps for her mother to come and visit when she was staying with her grandmother. This earliest memory stood as a metaphor for the core relational issues. There had been love between them, and she seemed more sad than depressed. This suggests a relatively well-established internal connection with a good-enough mother of the first three years, with a traumatic separation at that time. This memory can be understood as a metaphor as well, for the most salient aspect of her relationship with her mother. Not only was there the grief of missing and of yearning. There was likely a sense of the self as not enough to make Mother want to keep Isobel at home with her. It is this narcissistic wound and a diminished sense of self that would need repair. Keeping in mind the young child's ideas of causality and egocentric thinking, it would make sense to hypothesize that she explained the abandonments on the basis of something lacking in herself. In this manner, she could, to some extent, preserve the image of a good mother. However, the abandonment anger was revealed in her present-day entitlement claims.

What would repair the diminished sense of self? As a growing child, it was evident that a series of men had something she did not have, something that gave them access to mother in a way she did not have. Although at this point we begin to make hypotheses about the meaning of the Thunderbird and of the attraction to powerful males, and, although these hypotheses may or may not be borne out, nevertheless they indicate an avenue of exploration that will have to be undertaken. Does the powerful maleness that could control access to mother become a wished-for attribute of the self? Is there a grandiose self that is fed by a sense of borrowing the maleness of her powerful partners? Can she magically gain this by attaching herself to powerful womanizing men? Does her ability to capture the man by her sexuality defend against the feelings of powerlessness vis-à-vis the mother? And if the man wants her, is she not okay? When he turns to other women, is not the original narcissistic trauma replicated? Are not her relationships with men essentially dyadic and preoedipal in nature? We remember that there was no early attachment to a male figure despite the later attachment to her second stepfather. With this absence of an early father representation, we should not be misled into looking at her relationships with men as oedipal in nature. Where there was no early father attachment, there was no triangle during that phase of development.

Again, the principle of discovering the questions that need to be asked rather than belief in some ex-cathedra answer relieves the therapist of having to know. We may consider hypotheses that either will be confirmed by our exploration or will prove not to be on course. These hypotheses come from a combination of our understanding of the patient and of normal psychological development and what is either conducive to it or detrimental in its effect. For example, if we know that the patient was the middle child of three children who were born a year apart, and where the mother was the sole caregiver, it is not beyond probability that the earliest years were characterized by less than enough nurturant, stimulating, and holding interaction. In Isobel's case, what was indicated was the need for a careful and sensitive attention to the narcissistic vulnerability as well as a patient and careful uncovering of the complex dynamics of the situation. The therapist could expect an erotic transference to develop and would have to be ready to look at it with the patient in a manner that would not be narcissistically traumatizing. There would have to be a careful monitoring of the countertransference as Isobel would shift from the depressive and narcissistic issues clearly associated with the loss of Mother to that seductive erotic transference. The therapist noted at this point that there were already vestiges of this development in play. Interpretation would play a major role in the resolution of the acting-out defense.

The core relationship issue could be seen as emerging at the point of traumatic separation from mother, probably in the context of a less than secure attachment, albeit adequate to provide relative cohesion and differentiation. The developmental arrest could be located as in the latter stage of the separation-individuation process. Subsequent developmental stages would be condensed into the earlier object relations setup along with eroticism and sexuality. The most likely misdiagnosis in such a situation is that this is an oedipal patient and that the erotic transference with the male therapist is a father transference.

# CHAPTER 21

# Barbara: Grandiose Self-Defense

Barbara was a 49-year-old never-married woman. Her job was at the managerial level. She was very attractive, and it was important that she look sophisticated and stylish. Her presenting problem was chronic fatigue syndrome and depression. Despite the medical diagnosis, the sense of the therapist was that the complaints related to an inner emptiness and deadness.

The patient had been shopping for a therapist and had a history of many short-lived relationships as well as many short-lived therapies. At the first session, she indicated that she would probably go to a male therapist she had just interviewed. This therapist felt dismissed and a pressure to sell herself. In the next few sessions, the therapist became aware of how she herself was dressing on the day of Barbara's appointment, wanting to avoid any criticism from the patient. At the third session, Barbara commented that the therapist was not what she needed, that she needed someone on the cutting edge professionally. She compared the therapist unfavorably to another woman in the building who was described as younger and having more verve. The therapist was having difficulty stepping back from the sense of realness.

Barbara had been drawn to charismatic men. If they did not fit that description she got bored. On the other side of the coin, she was afraid that she would bore them. Boredom is often a consequence of emotional detachment or depression.

The history revealed that a younger sister had been born when Barbara was 2 years old and that, due to mother's poor health, Barbara was sent to live with relatives for some time. This was the developmental trauma that would shape subsequent development. She would be at the height of the felt dependency of the rapprochement phase of development. Later she recalled Father saying, "Be quiet. Don't upset your mother. You'll kill her." Once Mother was lost, there was no way to return to her.

Barbara felt that Mother wanted to mold her into some image in Mother's mind. That is, Mother did not support the unfolding of a true self. Barbara would continue to be reactive to her environment. Mother was seen as having all the power in the family. Father was described as a wimp, although he did take the children on trips and outings.

Mother would berate Father, and Barbara would go to the homes of friends frequently to get away from the mother.

Mother never was satisfied with Barbara, constantly criticizing her in all aspects. When we consider this in light of the transference–countertransference situation, we see the replication of the critical mother scenario with the roles reversed. The therapist comes to feel as Barbara quite likely felt vis-à-vis her mother. It would be important for the therapist to make use of this very unpleasant evoked countertransference, perhaps to note that Barbara seems to have turned the tables and does with the therapist as was done to her—that is, she replicates her relationship with her mother but with the roles reversed. If she seems able to work with this mild confrontation, it would be useful to say something like. "Let's try to understand this as motivated behavior, to see what important psychological function it serves for you." The therapist does not disclose the countertransference feelings but uses them to understand what Barbara is doing and to bring attention to what is going on in the transference dynamically. The meaning of the behavior needs to be uncovered, and inquiry opens the discovery process. It might prove to be a way for her to feel connected to her mother, to her internal object but with herself in the power position this time. She both acts out the wish for the mother and defends against the dangers of having her.

Barbara cannot stand the therapist's empathic responses, confronting the therapist with the paradox in which an empathic response is experienced as a failure of empathy. It would be important to understand what about the empathic response is dystonic, how she experiences it. Here again the importance of inquiry is demonstrated if we are to understand certain reactions. She adopts a tough "I don't need you" stance with the therapist as she had with her mother. With this rejection of dependency, we may hypothesize the existence of a grandiose self-defense, the transference situation described by Kohut (1971). When the idealized object fails to be perfect enough, the object is devalued, dismissed, viewed with contempt, and the grandiose self-defensive structure is mobilized. This flip can be pointed out as taking place again and again, accounting for the many aborted relationships. The very young child, turning away from needing the abandoning object, has little other recourse than an illusion of her own omnipotence. When this defense fails, she is thrust back into loss of all support, inner or outer, and falls into the emptiness and depression of that situation. There is likely to be a resistance to a dependent transference, inasmuch as depending on anyone is too dangerous. Yet, it is likely that traces of dependency will develop. With each inevitable disappointment she is likely to move quickly to the defensive posture.

Since this defensive maneuver is ego-syntonic, one must be careful not to reinforce it by an empathic response alone. If she is confronted with the psychological, emotional, and interpersonal costliness of the defense, hopefully it will become ego-dystonic, further motivating the hard work of therapy. That is, it is interpreted as a defense along with what it defends against, the loss of the good object. The excitement of the charismatic man enables the manic defense within the context of an interpersonal relationship. It brings the grandiose self into relationship. This is probably less a dependent relationship than it is a manifestation of a fusion with his power, making it her own. A truly dependent relationship is far too dangerous, as it would mean letting go of the grandiose self, manic defense. The grandiose self is essentially a schizoid posture in which the very existence of the object is denied, while the power of the object is condensed into the self.

Barbara instructed her therapist to "tell it to me straight. Don't tone down what you say." She herself does not want to be treated in a manner that might seem condescending and thus demeaning. It is likely that she will take well to interpretation that helps her make sense of her experience. The twin threads of interpersonal security versus insecurity, and pride versus shame, will wind through the work, and the therapist should be sensitive to these issues as they arise, combining that sensitivity with interpretation, keeping in mind the core relationship issue, the point of developmental derailment.

# CHAPTER 22

# Joshua: Noninvolvement

This 25-year-old man appeared to have a cohesive and well-differentiated self. His presenting problems concerning work and self-esteem were clearly related to the father–son relationship. His father was highly competitive with him, always needing to win, to be right, to be smarter. Joshua would only go so far in challenging his father, always aware that, beneath this "puffed-up" exterior, his father was very vulnerable. Joshua genuinely loved him and felt guilty at the thought of hurting him. By keeping himself "less than" in comparison with his father, his self-esteem was compromised and he then needed to puff himself up to compensate for the felt devaluation.

The relationship with the mother was largely positive, although he felt that she could be as dominating as the father in her own way. There was a great deal of affection between Joshua and his mother, a situation he felt the father resented. Joshua's earliest memory as reported at his first session was being scolded by his father for going into his mother's purse. Joshua was 3 or 4 at the time. He could not see the sexual implications of the memory if taken as metaphor, but was able to connect it with the father's resentment at his closeness with the mother.

This was a rather straightforward treatment of an oedipal patient, except for one issue that was played out in the transference.

From the age of 3 on, Joshua earned a specialness with his parents by virtue of his ready acceptance of the rules of proper social behavior. In essence, he learned to imitate the behaviors of the idealized parent figures. A source of pride was the fact that they would take him to fancy restaurants because he was so well behaved. Even as a young adult he took inordinate pride in knowing how to behave in elegant settings.

The therapist asked for consultation midway in his treatment inasmuch as something did not feel right in the process. This might have been viewed as a brief therapy case, but there was no anxiety as the interpretive work was done. Joshua seemed to pick up almost too quickly on the therapist's interventions. Yet, there was no sense of inner change.

Looking at the probable transference–countertransference situation, it seemed that he was "doing therapy" in accord with his learned approach to how to do life in general—through careful studying and modeling his behavior on that of the "adults." He called himself a "quick study." His quick, bright, and personable adaptation kept alive his feelings of specialness that came with being the chosen child and with being the oedipal winner at age 9 when his parents divorced. At the same time, his actual adult abilities did not contribute to his sense of competence, always feeling at the heart of it like a child doing something he had learned to do. This was not like the case of the as-if personality whose adaptation takes the place of what Giovacchini (1975) calls "the blank self." It was an adaptation in the service of the oedipal competition. He would be angry if his parents went out to dinner without him, feeling very insulted at being left out. The adaptive behavior was in the service of the specialness.

The therapist was able to see how she had gone along in a teaching mode in a counter-adaptation to his presentation of himself as bright student. With consistent interpretation of this adaptive strategy and the unconscious wishes and defenses contained within it, as well as the therapist's insistence on his doing the exploratory work more on his own, the treatment moved forward to a full exploration of the complex relationship with his father and its resolution. He was able to make and follow through on autonomous decisions, even when they might run contrary to what his father wanted him to do. He also turned less to his mother as confidante and was no longer at her beck and call. He acted more decisively in his business and with far less anxiety about taking charge of the situation.

This is a good example of how the clue to therapeutic impasse is most often found within the relational setup between patient and therapist.

# CHAPTER 23

# Marie: Total Control of the Process

This 33-year-old woman had been in twice-weekly psychotherapy for seven months. She worked as an entertainer. Her opening comment at the start of treatment was, "Thank God I'm back in therapy." Her therapy history was mixed. She felt destroyed by the first, conjoint therapy with a live-in boyfriend. She felt that the therapist had tried to fill her with bad stuff. The second experience with a pastoral counselor had been positive and supportive.

The father was an alcoholic, and the household

revolved around him. He did earn some respect in the outer world. Mother served him in a saint-like way, giving up her own career in order to serve him. She also elevated his position. The extent of the father's insensitivity to the needs of others was manifest in his spending hours in the only bathroom. The patient felt she was almost forced to wet the bed. If Marie had an opinion about anything, the father would tell her not to be so smart. He would ridicule her intelligence. Despite this, she tried desperately to be his little girl.

Mother's position was characterized as one of exalted sainthood, and in nothing Marie did could she be as good as Mother.

Marie felt that her role with everyone was to fill up their ego needs. The question was whether she should be self-interested or other-interested.

The youngest of five children, Marie felt adequately mothered until she entered kindergarten. At that time, she felt sent off and abandoned. She learned to be a brave little soldier, a posture that was now her persona. She attracted people by being solid and pleasing.

The presenting therapist felt that he should help, but felt overwhelmed. Marie would fill the sessions with many stories, and the therapist did not have any sense of what they were about or what to pick up on anymore. If he said anything, she would experience it as disruptive, even if he were supportive. If he said anything at all, she would become agitated. It was very likely that he was experiencing the same kind of existential annihilation experienced by the patient in her growing-up years, when even her basic needs had to take second place to the demands and entitlements of the father and the mother's support of him. She had developed a false self, the pleasing little soldier, but was not bringing this into the transference. Quite the opposite: she was bringing the angry child who was now demanding what she had been forced to give—total attention and indulgence. Any intervention by the therapist was tantamount to a demand. She would have to hear him and react to him. As long as the therapist tried to work with the content of the stories, the interpersonal process issue was lost.

Marie reported a long-term relationship. It broke up because *she* would not commit. She also reported painful intercourse because of vaginismus. Because of this, her current relationship was now in jeopardy. In effect, she was not letting the therapist in, either, and whatever commitment she was making, it was on the grounds of her having total control of the process.

The transference resistance—that is, the management of the therapy relationship so as to prevent the therapist's taking her over—would first have to be interpreted. The interpretation would have to be done empathically, with a sensitive understanding of how she must feel the need to protect her very survival, to protect herself from the therapist's taking her over in the service of his needs as the parents had done. This would address the core relationship conflict—the wish to be connected but the fear of it as well, and the strategies she used to defend herself as well as the negative outcome of those strategies. Her comment at the start of treatment, "Thank God I'm back in therapy," expressed the interpersonal wish; the transference resistance revealed the fear. The need–fear dilemma would have to be spelled out. As she would come to feel the therapist's understanding of her dilemma, hopefully she would begin to feel safe enough to begin the painful process of uncovering and eventually, of working through.

With respect to character structure, the feeling was that

there was a cohesive self. The years before kindergarten were remembered as good enough. Since she was the youngest child, she did not have to lose the mother to a later-born sibling. Things seemed to go awry with her individuation and the emergence of her own abilities, intelligence, and talents. As she would threaten to upstage the parents, she was promptly put in her place, so to speak. The therapist's felt sense of inadequacy was quite likely a concordant counter-transference, the therapist's experiencing of what Marie was made to experience vis-à-vis the envious and competitive parents. The presence of a cohesive self and the core conflict's arising beyond the preoedipal period should give the therapist greater latitude in making interpretations. Despite the defense against being dominated and over-whelmed by the demands of the other, Marie was not in danger of a dissolution of the self if the therapist took an interpretive initiative. Her oedipal strivings, the attempts to be daddy's little girl, further attest to her progress into that developmental phase. However, the intense enmeshment of the parents left little room for her to achieve any degree of felt success in these strivings. Her feelings around these issues would be able to come forth in the uncovering stage once the initial transference resistance was interpreted and adequately resolved.

# CHAPTER 24

## Gary: Fear of Annihilation

This 21-year-old college senior had been seen briefly by the therapist when Gary was in fifth grade. His first male teacher, who stood in stark contrast with the supportive female teachers of his early grades, created so much anxiety in Gary that he became "school phobic." Brief intervention with the parents who had him transferred to a different class, enabled Gary to resume attending school.

Parents were upper-middle-class, high-achieving individuals who expected the same level of performance of their children that they demanded of themselves. Gary's mother called the therapist expressing her concern at Gary's critical attitude toward himself and his uncertainty and ambivalence with respect to any further education.

When Gary finally called to make an appointment, he presented himself as closed off, uncomfortable about coming to therapy. He denied that there was any problem with having to conform to parental expectations. He only responded to direct questions. He did express some anxiety about what to do but denied he felt pressure from his parents, although they did want him to go to medical school. He was clearly resistant to that idea.

With some prodding, the therapist got him to say something about what *his* interests were. He mentioned something vague about music and said he might like to study history, to find out what the world was all about. In consultation, this statement was regarded as a metaphor and the only thing Gary revealed about his private experience. It was taken to indicate his confusion about his own personal history, his confusion with what the world as he experienced it was all about. This coincided with the therapist's gut feeling that there "wasn't anyone home," that there was a blankness about Gary, that he was a blob. At the time of the session, the therapist did not pick up on this metaphor but went on to try to engage him, asking how it was to grow up in his family. She met with a wall of resistance. She commented to Gary that it must be difficult to acknowledge any negative feelings to parents who were as consistently good and generous as his were. However, he became increasingly guarded when asked further about his relationships. He had difficulty having girlfriends. His only spontaneous offering was in response to the outbreak of the Persian Gulf war. He said he would be scared but would be ready to go and that he would not go to Canada to evade any draft as his mother indicated she would want. This assertion of readiness for justifiable aggression reminds us of the importance of aggression in the separation–individuation process, that is, the child's ability to push against and push away from mother in the service of that process. He was, however, afraid to get a job.

He missed one session because of traffic, and the last time he came in (a total of eight meetings), he didn't want to talk. Whatever early contact that the therapist felt was left from his positive memory of their sessions when he was a child was gone. His mother called to cancel his next appointment.

At this point, the therapist was not sure she even had a patient, but wanted to have a direction to follow should he return to see her. The following thoughts were based on the material as presented above, as a hypothesis that would be worth following, addressing the resistance to the process.

It was suggested that his interest in history as metaphor be interpreted, that he was confused as to what the world was about in large part because his parents had always defined reality for him in terms of their own beliefs, values, and ambitions—that is, his true self was annihilated within the family system. If this were so, he would surely be afraid that the therapist would do the same thing—that she would pose a threat of existential annihilation. His way of being had been to adapt to his environment, and therapy could be experienced as a danger to the core intrinsic self that he probably was not even consciously aware of. The therapist experienced his passive defensive and withholding posture, which frustrated her. Erikson's (1950) concept of identity diffusion comes to mind here. Faced with any extreme change in his external environment, such as that experienced with his fifth grade teacher, or with his upcoming graduation from college, found him without a core self to enable him to negotiate such changes. The cognitive elaboration of his dilemma and the source of his anxiety, and the therapist's empathic understanding of his attempts to protect himself, hopefully would recall the earlier alliance.

If Gary did not return, it was suggested that the therapist write him a note asking him to come for at least one more session, and if he did so, the core issue could be put forth, at least giving the treatment a chance by addressing the major resistance at the outset.

# CHAPTER 25

# Harvey: Idealizing the Authority Figure

The therapist presented this patient because of his (the therapist's) sense of helplessness and confusion in the situation. Harvey was a 40-year-old successful journalist. His presenting problem was his panic and hysteria at his daughter's chronic bronchitis and attacks of croup at night.

Harvey pictured himself as a fat, nonathletic boy when he was a child, who suffered repeated humiliations in sports situations. He developed other channels to compensate for this felt inferiority by being entertaining and a ladies' man when he was older.

Both of Harvey's parents were heavy smokers, and the sound of coughing haunted his childhood. He was sure they would die when he heard them coughing, especially at night. His mother died at the age of 62.

His two siblings were older and essentially out of the house during his preteen and teen years. Left alone at night frequently, he would anxiously await someone's return, unable to sleep until then.

Harvey described his father as cold. Harvey was angry that his father never taught him how to be a boy and how to be athletic. He pursued his father's approval, which he did not feel was ever forthcoming. However, the father would watch TV and talk with him. That is, he would join him in his passivity.

The mother was hypochondriacal, obsessed with health concerns. Although Harvey described her as warm and nurturing, he also said she was not emotionally involved. She was full of drama and hysteria, dispensed various medications to everyone, and was involved mostly in her relationships with her doctors. She clearly idealized them and depended on them. That is, she turned to her physicians for her most important object relationships.

Harvey felt warm and safe with a housekeeper who was very nice to him, but when he was about 12 years old he decided she was stupid and turned away from her. Harvey also had more recently turned away from his wife, who disappointed him by not maintaining the same competent professional image that she had presented when they first met.

Looking at the transference–countertransference situation, we learn that Harvey twice stopped treatment and then returned. Although he presented a lot of material, there did not seem to be any interest in exploring its meaning. There seemed to be no psychological motivation. While the therapist felt helpless and confused, he also felt vaguely uncomfortable at the way Harvey used his title, putting "Dr. XX" into his communications frequently. When his wife wanted his support, Harvey tended to give authoritative answers, as though he were "the doctor" under these circumstances.

The "doctor transference" appeared to be the only entree to understanding what was going on in the process. If we think how the mother herself seemed to rely on doctors for her own emotional support and calming, unable to contain her easily mobilized anxiety, we can hypothesize that she was unable to contain and modulate Harvey's emotional distresses when he was very small. We see how, as an adult, he is as enamored of doctors as she was. With no internal soothing mechanisms as a consequence of the mother's inability to contain and to soothe, Harvey also turns hysterically to the authority who is expected to heal his distress, often presented in the form of a somatic disorder. We see the pattern repeated with his own child who is being greeted with parental hysteria when her respiratory problems panic him. It does not require any great leap to predict that his relationship to his therapist is predicated upon the same kind of emotional reliance as upon the medical doctors he turns to. This is one of those situations in which being in therapy is, in effect, an acting out. There is no observing ego, and no working alliance. Material is presented in much the same way as his list of symptoms is anxiously presented to his physicians. It would be necessary to interpret these dynamics, hopefully to enlist Harvey's interest in a psychological approach to his problems.

Harvey's readiness to idealize (the maid and his wife),

and his readiness to reject when that idealization fails, alert us to the probability of an underlying character pathology entailing splitting. He does not appear to have a grandiose self as a defensive fallback position, but instead is overwhelmed with anxiety, which is often expressed in somatic symptoms. It is unclear from the material presented whether he is able to experience affect as a qualitatively specific experience, or whether all affect is reduced to psychophysiological distress: that is, that he suffered from alexithymia (see page 189). In view of Harvey's mother's proclivity to drama and hysteria, it is likely that she was not able to help her son develop the capacity to differentiate and correctly label various affect states.

# CHAPTER 26

# Charlie: Compulsive Acting Out

This 35-year-old man was troubled by his compulsive sexual behaviors and by his obsessive thoughts about sex. He was the middle child of three children. His brother, who was older by 11 years, was given responsibility for taking care of the young Charlie. Charlie, in turn, had to take care of the youngest child.

Charlie portrayed his mother as a power monster who made slaves of the rest of the family, especially Charlie. If he didn't do what she wanted she would hit him, and if he tried to defend himself he would be attacked for that. The intrusive mother often attacked the passive alcoholic father. The children were challenged to say which parent they would want to live with in case of a divorce. The general atmosphere was chaotic, with no boundaries. Closed doors were not allowed. There was a general negligence with respect to diet and medical or dental care. In general, Charlie was left with feelings of emptiness and profound deprivation.

Charlie described himself as a "nerd" at school. He was not athletic and was usually the last chosen in school yard games. From childhood on he seemed to have a tentative hold on reality, constructing fantasies as a substitute. He always yearned for and fantasied having the ideal "Norman Rockwell family" and with heroic denial has tried to convince himself that this is possible with his family. He used marijuana to get himself into adulthood, to help him feel good enough so that he could negotiate his daily life.

Charlie's work consists of a series of projects that consume him, with a collapse at the completion of each project. He tried to curb his sexual acting out when he married but was unable to resist the obsessive and compulsive pressures. He experienced guilt at his pleasure when viewing a porno movie in which the woman was forced to do what the man wanted, realizing that he had been the victim vis-à-vis his mother's power. That is, the power he felt in the identification with the aggressor was highly eroticized (Horner 1989).

Charlie had been in therapy for several months. His therapist wanted to be able to formulate the basic issues so as to work most effectively. He didn't feel that Charlie related to him as a person and felt invisible, much like a priest in the confessional. Charlie's torment was palpable.

As with any obsession or with a compulsive acting out, one asks, "What is the psychological function of the symptom? Why is it necessary?" As we can construct a sense of the internalized chaos that would evolve out of the early interpersonal matrix, Charlie would have to find a way to contain and bind anxiety and a way to give him a sense of himself as existing. For Charlie, the issues are primarily existential, with a constant fight against the terror of annihilation of the self. How can he convince himself that he exists? The use of the body is often the only anchor in the presence of this kind of annihilation terror. Charlie felt very powerful after a sexual experience, but as a chronically needed antidote to feelings of terror and nonexistence, his symptoms were in the nature of an addiction that could quiet his fears but not resolve them.

The penis is a very important organizer for the little boy's sense of maleness. He can see it. He can feel it. And it is a clear indication that he is, indeed, a boy. The psychological importance of the penis and its sexual activities in adult pathology depend on the nature of the underlying character structure, the organization of the self. Compulsive sexual behavior can affirm to the patient (1) I exist, (2) I am male, or (3) I am a potent male. The analytic work should clarify the specific meanings for this specific patient.

Both the sexual behaviors and the highs associated with his work were in the nature of a manic defense. Because of the intensely intrusive and assaultive quality of his early environment, he couldn't develop useful schizoid defenses. There could be no closed doors in the house or in his psyche. He tried to construct a fantasy ideal family, knowing what he needed for his own growth and development, but a child cannot develop a healthy structure based on fantasy alone.

It is likely that the primary structures that evolved out

of the primary caretaking matrix are as chaotic and probably psychotic as the matrix itself. This would be the kind of situation that Kohut would characterize as requiring the building of compensatory structures over a basically irreparable primary structure, those new structures to evolve over a long period of therapy with the therapist who can function in a way that will enable the emergence and consolidation of a sense of self as cohesive and real. Interpreting to the patient his core existential struggle and helping him understand the behaviors that trouble him in light of this struggle should give Charlie a way of organizing his experience, of being able to express it in words, and should connect him with the therapist through the latter's empathic understanding of what that struggle is.

# Epilogue

## ASKING THE RIGHT QUESTIONS

When students and supervisees struggle to find the "right answer," I usually suggest that it is more important to ask the right question, to join the patient in a project of exploration and discovery in the context of a safe and supporting relationship.

The most important resource you have is your-self—your own ability to listen, to feel, to intuit, and to synthesize, as well as your own humanity and good will.

The most important preparation you can make is to know yourself, to have no dark recesses of the mind you are afraid to enter, to deny no dark side of the soul. The ability to face yourself nonjudgmentally and nondefensively will make it possible to help your patient do the same.

Ultimately, we all hope to achieve a solid and valued sense of self even as we yearn for intimacy and committed and authentic relating. A successful course of psychoanalytic psychotherapy is one route to that goal, although surely not the only one.

## THE ROLE OF WORK IN THE THERAPIST'S LIFE

Although having a fulfilling life with emotionally gratifying relationships outside of the world of work is not a prerequisite for licensing as a psychotherapist, the absence of these factors should alert the therapist to the potential for overvaluing his or her role and for overvaluing certain therapist–patient relationships.

While many patients report an illusion of being or the wish to be the therapist's favorite patient, when this is, in fact, the case, the patient is at a serious disadvantage. There is likely to be a transference–countertransference collusion to avoid anything that would destroy the positive and gratifying ambience. The treatment is almost sure to be compromised as a consequence.

Therapists who find too much gratification in their role as helper may unconsciously reinforce regressive behaviors that are in the service of defense. While becoming a therapist may represent a sublimation of an earlier gratifying helper role assignment within the family, with true sublimation, the need-gratification aspect of helping has been adequately relinquished and transformed to healthy goals and ideals. As such, the patient's emergence as a self-sufficient individual will be welcomed by the therapist rather than being experienced as a rejection or abandonment.

The importance of developing other sectors of the personality and of building a life beyond work should not be lost in the intense and sometimes frenzied educational and training process. It is an essential antidote to the development of too great a sense of preciousness about one's work, one's professional self, and one's therapeutic relationships.

To be allowed into the private spaces of the self by our patients is a privilege as well as a responsibility. Ultimately, it enlarges the horizons of our views of human existence. It opens a window to many different ways of being, some frightening, some inspiring, yet all worthy of both our interest and our respect.

# APPENDIX

## Syllabus

In this section, I present a collection of readings that provide a guide through the literature for the reader who wants to broaden his or her education in the area of psychoanalytic therapy. These references are relevant to a variety of clinical situations.

1. Michael Balint, Chapters 3, 4, and 5, in *The Basic Fault* (London: Tavistock, 1968).

Here Balint makes a distinction among the three areas of the mind. Area 3 is the area of the Oedipus conflict. It is characterized by the fact that everything that happens involves at least two parallel objects in addition to the subject. Area 2 is the area of the basic fault. In it only two people are involved—the preoedipal dyad. Although highly dynamic, the force originating from the basic fault is not in the form of a conflict. It has the form of a fault, or something distorted or lacking in the mind. Area 1 is the area of creation. In it there is no outside object involved. Thus, there is no object relationship and no transference. Balint describes the manifestation of these areas of the mind in the treatment process.

2. Peter Blos, "Son and father," *Journal of the American Psychoanalytic Association,* 1984, vol. 32, pp. 301–324.

Blos conceptualizes the normal developmental progression in male personality formation with explicit reference to the fate of the boy's dyadic father relationship—that is, the relationship with the preoedipal father—as well as the relationship with the father of the Oedipus complex. Self-defeating defenses such as the sabotaging of success of the male oedipal patient often relate to the love for the father established in the earlier years and the wish to preserve that aspect of the dyadic father–son relationship.

3. Christopher Bollas, Chapter 7 in *The Shadow of the Object: Psychoanalysis of the Unthought Known* (New York: Columbia University Press, 1987).

Bollas describes relationships characterized by "loving hate." He sees its aim as a wish to get closer to the object, with a surrender to affect. He notes that the outcome of a psychic activity does not necessarily define its intention. Therapists often assume that it does define intention and seriously misread the patient. That is, a person who is drawn toward being hateful and who cultivates the passion of hate may actually be showing a perverse object relation. It represents a *wish for* a relationship in that event.

4. Christopher Bollas, "The transformational object," *International Journal of Psycho-Analysis,* 1978, vol. 60, pp. 97–107.

Bollas says that the infant's other self, the mother, continually transforms the infant's internal and external environment. The search for the transformational object in adult life is a recognition of the need for ego repair. Bollas relates this to certain clinical situations.

5. Walter Burke and Michael Tansey, "Projective identification and countertransference turmoil: disruptions in the empathic process," *Contemporary Psychoanalysis,* 1985, vol. 21, pp. 372–393.

The authors describe the empathic process from (1) reception to (2) internal processing and (3) communication. They describe the effect of the patient's use of projective identification on the therapist's ability to complete all the phases of the empathic process. This paper is especially helpful for the therapist who is experiencing this countertransference distress induced by such a patient.

6. Roy Calogeras and Toni Alston, "Family pathology and the infantile neurosis," *International Journal of Psycho-Analysis,* 1985, vol. 66, pp. 359–373.

The writers describe the situation in which the pathological family milieu has succeeded in providing a certain "critical state" for the maintenance of the childhood in adulthood, and how it is a major inhibiting force in the failure to resolve the pathology. It is important for the therapist who works with the psychoanalytic model to understand the developmental implications of the pathological family system and to understand that what we see clinically at times is the patient's adaptation to that system, an adaptation that has pathological sequellae. To interpret these sequellae from the point of view of a one-person psychology will constitute a serious failure to understand the person.

7. R. Horacio Etchegoyen, Benito Lopez, and Moses Rabih, "On envy and how to interpret it," *International Journal of Psycho-Analysis,* 1987, vol. 68, pp. 49–61.

The authors present their argument for the prompt interpretation of envy as soon as it appears, as well as their suggestions for how to interpret it. Envy of the therapist may constitute the source of major transference resistances. To allow therapy to succeed may be experienced as an acknowledgment of the power of the therapist, which is then envied and must be spoiled.

8. Jay R. Greenberg, "Theoretical models and the analyst's neutrality," *Contemporary Psychoanalysis,* 1986, vol. 22, pp. 87–106.

Greenberg defines neutrality in relational terms, as optimal tension between the patient's experience of us as old or new objects. This position is a reference point for monitoring our technique in any given treatment. He does *not* see neutrality as others do, as nonresponsiveness, anonymity, colorlessness, or nonalignment. It is unique for each individual. One person's neutrality is another's abandonment.

9. Ralph Greenson, Disidentifying from mother: its special importance for the boy, in *Explorations in Psychoanalysis* (New York: International Universities Press, 1968).

This is a seminal paper on gender identity development in the boy. It makes clear why gender identity disorders occur primarily in males. Object relations development is impacted by this developmental switch point for the little boy. The little girl does not have this same hurdle to overcome. Any tendency to view development in unisex terms or to interpret this action by the boy simply as a response to social–cultural pressures will lead to a serious misunderstanding of the adult male patient who has identity conflicts originating from this phase of development.

10. Ralph Greenson, "Loving, hating and indifference towards the patient," *International Review of Psycho-Analysis,* 1974, vol. 1, pp. 259–266.

Greenson's aim in this paper is to overcome confusions and the prejudice against acknowledging the constructive potential of the countertransference. More recent writers have developed this concept further and that prejudice has declined.

11. James Grotstein, "Nothingness, meaninglessness, chaos, and the 'black hole,' " I., *Contemporary Psychoanalysis,* 1990, vol. 26, pp. 257–290.

Although this is a difficult paper to read, it is well worth the effort inasmuch as it sheds important light on certain traumatic states sometimes reported by the patient. It relates to the dissolution of the internal world within which the self and sense of self are structured and the defenses erected against this experience. Developmentally, this would relate to those times of early infancy when the caretaking environment fails in its holding capacity and when there is, as yet, no permanent internal object to sustain the self at those times. It is important to be able to work with these concepts when they are relevant to any given patient's experience.

12. Mark Grunes, "The therapeutic object relationship," *Psychoanalytic Review,* 1984, vol. 71, pp. 123–143.

Grunes views the therapeutic object relationship as the core of the psychoanalytic process and as the curative matrix of treatment. It is also defined as organically interrelated to transference and interpretation.

13. Harry Guntrip, Chapter 6 in *Psychoanalytic Theory, Therapy, and the Self* (New York: Basic Books, 1971).

Guntrip writes that the complex pattern of ego-splitting or loss of primary psychic unity is the root cause of personality disorders in later life. The most vulnerable part of the self is the most hidden part. To reach and help the lost heart of the personal self is the profoundest problem posed for psychotherapy.

14. Irwin Hirsch, "Varying modes of analytic participation," *Journal of the American Academy of Psychoanalysis,* 1987, vol. 15, pp. 205–222.

The key to change involves helping the patient see the conflict between pulls toward the old patterns of interpersonal relating and the potential of a new one while unwittingly falling into these old patterns and making these patterns explicit as they reach awareness.

15. Althea Horner, "The 'real' relationship and analytic neutrality," *Journal of the American Academy of Psychoanalysis,* 1987, vol. 15, pp. 491–501.

This paper addresses the question, "How does who we are in the treatment situation cast its shadow on the final outcome of treatment just as powerfully as what we do?" How can we provide a genuine curative matrix without jeopardizing neutrality as Greenberg defines it?

16. Althea Horner, "The constructed self and developmental discontinuity," *Journal of the American Academy of Psychoanalysis,* 1988, vol. 16, pp. 235–238.

A relative of the false self, the constructed self evolves as a defense against intolerable shame and self-hatred and is shaped in accord with a fantasied ego ideal. It is not grandiose in the usual sense of the term, but it must be perfect lest the shame erupt again in full force. The important distinction between this and the false self is made. Empathic interpretation of the defense is critical lest the treatment process itself become subsumed within the constructed self, in which case the treatment has, as an unconscious aim, the perfection of the constructed self.

17. Otto Kernberg, "Projection and projective identification: developmental and clinical aspects," *Journal of the American Psychoanalytic Association Monograph,* 1986, pp. 795–819.

Projective identification and projection are defined, described, and contrasted. Projective identification is a fundamental source of information about the patient and requires an active utilization of the analyst's countertransference responses in order to elaborate the interpretation of this mechanism in the transference.

18. Melanie Klein, Our adult world and its roots in infancy, in *Envy and Gratitude and Other Works* (New York: Delacorte, 1959).

Klein writes that if we look at our adult world from the viewpoint of its roots in infancy, we gain insight into the way our mind, habits, and views have been built up from the earliest infantile fantasies and emotions to the most complex and sophisticated adult manifestations. Nothing that ever existed in the unconscious completely loses its influence on the personality. This is an important point even if we do not agree entirely with Klein's vision of the world of the infant.

19. Heinz Kohut, Chapter 1, in *The Analysis of the Self* (New York: International Universities Press, 1971).

This chapter sets out schematically the core narcissistic transferences and their dynamic relationships. Whether or not one subscribes to a self psychology theory of treatment, this early clinical work of Kohut is extremely useful when the therapist is confronted by these shifting transferences.

20. Hans Loewald, "Oedipus complex and the development of self," *Psychoanalytic Quarterly,* 1985, vol. 54, pp. 435–443.

Loewald notes that the emergence of oedipal object relations—that is, the capacity for triadic rather than only dyadic relations—is a crucial stage in the development toward adult mentation. Seen in the light of individuation, of the development of a self, and of objects related to but distinct from the self, the oedipal phase is a crucial turning point. By understanding this as a genuine step in his human development, the patient can move beyond being a victim of the selfobject stage and its narcissism.

21. Hans Loewald, "Transference–countertransference," *Journal of the American Psychoanalytic Association,* 1986, vol. 34, pp. 275–288.

Loewald discusses the dynamics of transference–countertransference as they reveal themselves in object relations and specifically in the treatment process. Loewald notes that transference and countertransference cannot be viewed separately and that they are normal ingredients of the therapeutic process. As others are coming to believe more and more, understanding one's own countertransference is important in the understanding of the patient. The therapist's self-knowledge is essential in order to be able to discern the immediate interpersonal significance of his or her own reactions.

22. Stephen Mitchell, "The wings of Icarus: illusion and the problem of narcissism," *Contemporary Psychoanalysis,* 1986, vol. 22, pp. 107–132.

Mitchell notes that illusions of self-sufficiency and perfection of the grandiose self undercut the basic premise of the treatment process, that the patient might gain something useful from another person. There are differences of opinion as to the management of such illusions. Some argue that illusions must be interpreted vigorously and quickly, their unreality pointed out, and their defensive purpose explored. Others write as cogently about the importance of the therapist's empathic support of illusions, since this is what the patient is actually experiencing and as such is closest to his or her real self. Mitchell comes to a synthesizing approach in which the therapist's participation is essential to the establishment of the patient's integration, while the therapist's questioning of illusions is essential to their dissolution and the capacity for a richer form of relationship.

23. Fred Pine, "On the pathology of the separation-individuation process as manifested in later clinical work," *International Journal of Psycho-Analysis,* 1979, vol. 60, pp. 225–242.

Pine makes a very useful distinction between pathology that involves the relation to the differentiated other versus pathology that involves the relation to the *undifferentiated* other. He distinguishes low- and high-level pathology of separation–individuation, the former having to do with the undifferentiated other and high-level pathology having to do with the differentiated other but *tied to the differentiation process itself.* It is because of such subtle but critical distinctions that we cannot make across-the-board conclusions about the diagnostic group that might include both sets of patients or about how to work with them clinically.

24. Anne-Marie Sandler, "On the significance of Piaget's work for psychoanalysis," *International Review of Psycho-Analysis,* 1975, vol. 2, pp. 365–377.

Sandler refers to Piaget's study of the development of the child's concepts of causality, number, space, time, language, chance, speed, and so on. It is important for the therapist to keep in mind that the patient's memory and belief system was laid down when the individual was at a more primitive level of cognitive development. One aspect of the treatment process is to subject the child's version of its world to the mature cognitive abilities of the patient. The working alliance depends on these mature abilities. The child's egocentric perception of reality is especially significant in this respect and may in some way be related to a still-existing illusion of the ability to control.

25. Joseph Sandler, "Unconscious wishes and human relationships," *Contemporary Psychoanalysis,* 1981, vol. 17, pp. 180–196.

Sandler addresses the issue of motivation, the unconscious forces that affect behavior. He notes that the content of a wish normally includes a representation of the self and of the object in interaction. He emphasizes that the individual does not necessarily seek a replica of what he or she experienced in childhood. There is a need to obtain forms of actualization of the wish that are acceptable to the conscience and to the person's sense of reality. Thus, he is likely to disguise and distort the role relationships he wants to impose on others, while the needs of others force him to create and accept compromises. Nevertheless, Sandler points out, these unconscious wishes will profoundly affect the individual's relationship with others. Of course, this will take place in the therapeutic relationship as well, where it then becomes available for analysis and, ultimately, change.

26. Samuel Slipp, The symbiotic survival pattern: a relational theory of schizophrenia (*Family Process,* 1973), vol. 12, pp. 377–397.

The symbiotic survival pattern is found in families in which one individual feels responsible for the self-esteem and survival of another. Slipp describes the impact of such a pathological family system on the development of the internal world of the individual. Slipp works toward the integration of systems theory and object relations theory.

27. Paul Watzlawick, Janet Beavin, and Don Jackson, *The Pragmatics of Human Communication* (New York: Norton, 1967).

Although this work is not written from a psychoanalytic point of view, it is extremely useful in the understanding of the developmental impact of pathological communicational styles in the dysfunctional family. It is also helpful for the therapist who is faced with the patient's use of pathological communicational styles.

28. Donald Winnicott, Chapter 6, Ego distortion in terms of true and false self, in *The Maturational Processes and the Facilitating Environment* (New York: International Universities Press, 1965).

This most important paper deals with the child's adaptations to its caretaking environment that lead to a distortion of identity referred to as the "False Self." It is especially relevant to the treatment process, inasmuch as when the patient relates to the therapist through this false adaptational self, the treatment will fail. The first thing to be confronted and interpreted is the false self and how it is manifest in the treatment situation, along with an empathic understanding of how the child developed this strategy in the service of his or her own survival.

29. Donald Winnicott, "Fear of breakdown," *International Review of Psycho-Analysis,* 1975, vol. 1, pp. 103–107.

Winnicott notes that the patient's fear of breakdown in effect represents a memory of something that happened in infancy, although it cannot truly be "remembered" because there was no capacity to conceptualize it at that time. Winnicott notes that the need to experience it in treatment is equivalent to the need to remember in the analysis of psychoneurosis.

The following books by this author discuss theoretical and clinical issues consistent with the point of view of this book.

*Object Relations and the Developing Ego in Therapy,* 2nd ed. (New York: Jason Aronson, 1984).

*Treating the Oedipal Patient in Brief Psychotherapy* (New York: Jason Aronson, 1985).

*The Wish for Power and the Fear of Having It* (Northvale, NJ: Jason Aronson, 1989).

*Being and Loving,* 3rd ed. (Northvale, NJ: Jason Aronson, 1990).

*The Primacy of Structure: The Psychotherapy of Underlying Character Pathology* (Northvale, NJ: Jason Aronson, 1991).

# References

Abend, S. (1990). The psychoanalytic process: motives and obstacles in the search for clarification. *Psychoanalytic Quarterly* 59:532–549.

Adler, M. (1980). *How to Think About God*. New York: Bantam Books.

Arlow, J., and Brenner, C. (1990). The psychoanalytic process. *The Psychoanalytic Quarterly* 59:678–692.

Balint, M. (1968). *The Basic Fault*. London: Tavistock.

Bion, W. R. (1959). *Experiences in Groups and Other Papers*. New York: Basic Books.

______ (1977). *The Seven Servants.* New York: Jason Aronson.

Blos, P. (1984). Son and father. *Journal of the American Psychoanalytic Association* 32:301–324.

Boesky, D. (1990). The psychoanalytic process and its components. *The Psychoanalytic Quarterly* 59:550–584.

Bollas, C. (1978). The transformational object. *International Journal of Psycho-Analysis* 60:97–107.

______ (1987). *The Shadow of the Object: Psychoanalysis of the Unthought Known.* New York: Columbia University Press.

Buie, D., and Adler, G. (1973). The uses of confrontation in psychotherapy of borderline patients. In *Confrontation in Psychotherapy,* ed. G. Adler and P. Myerson, pp. 125–162. New York: Science House.

Burke, W., and Tansey, M. (1985). Projective identification and countertransference turmoil: disruptions in the empathic process. *Contemporary Psychoanalysis* 21:372–393.

Calogeras, R., and Alston, T. (1985). Family pathology and the infantile neurosis. *International Journal of Psycho-Analysis* 66:359–373.

Chess, S., and Thomas, A. (1977). *Temperament and Development.* New York: Brunner/Mazel.

Coates, S. (1990). Ontogenesis of boyhood gender identity disorder. *Journal of the American Academy of Psychoanalysis* 18:414–438.

Cooper, A. (1990). The future of psychoanalysis: challenges and opportunities. *Psychoanalytic Quarterly* 59:177–196.

Corwin, H. (1973). Therapeutic confrontation from routine to heroic. In *Confrontation in Psychotherapy,* ed. G. Adler and P. Myerson, pp. 69–95. New York: Science House.

Dewald, P. (1982). The clinical importance of the termination phase. *Psychoanalytic Inquiry* 2:441–461.

Eissler, K. R. (1974). On some theoretical and technical problems regarding the payment of fees for psychoanalytic treatment. *International Review of Psycho-Analysis* 1:73–102.

Epstein, L. (1982). Adapting to the patient's therapeutic need in the psychoanalytic situation. *Contemporary Psychoanalysis* 18:190–217.

Erikson, E. (1950). *Childhood and Society*. New York: Norton.

Etchegoyen, R. H. (1982). The relevance of the "here and now" transference interpretation for the reconstruction of early psychic development. *International Journal of Psycho-Analysis* 63:65–75.

Etchegoyen, R. H., Lopez, B., and Rabih, M. (1987). On envy and how to interpret it. *International Journal of Psycho-Analysis* 68:49–61.

Fantz, R. L. (1966). Pattern discrimination and selective attention as determinants of perceptual development from birth. In *Perceptual Development in Children,* ed. A. J. Kidd and J. L. Rivoire, pp. 143–173. New York: International Universities Press.

Frederickson, J. (1990). Hate in the countertransference as an empathic position. *Contemporary Psychoanalysis* 26:479–496.

Freud, A. (1946). *The Ego and the Mechanisms of Defense.* New York: International Universities Press.

______ (1954). The widening scope of indications for psychoanalysis. In *Writings,* vol. 4, pp. 356–376. New York: International Universities Press, 1968.

Freud, S. (1900). *The interpretation of dreams. Standard Edition* 4/5.

______ (1910). The future prospects of psychoanalytic theory. *Standard Edition* 11:141–151.

______ (1912a). Recommendations to physicians practicing psychoanalysis. *Standard Edition* 12:111–120.

______ (1912b). The dynamics of transference. *Standard Edition* 12:99–108.

_______ (1913). On beginning the treatment. (Further recommendations on the technique of psychoanalysis. I.) *Standard Edition* 12:123–144.

_______ (1917). Mourning and melancholia. *Standard Edition* 14:249.

_______ (1923a). The ego and the id. *Standard Edition* 19:12–59.

_______ (1923b). The dependent relationships of the ego. *Standard Edition* 19:48–59.

_______ (1933a). The dissection of the psychical personality. *Standard Edition* 22:57–80.

_______ (1933b). New introductory lectures on psychoanalysis. *Standard Edition* 22:155.

_______ (1937). Analysis terminable and interminable. *Standard Edition* 23:216–253.

Friedman, M. (1976). *Martin Buber: The Life of Dialogue.* 3rd revised ed. Chicago, IL: University of Chicago Press

Ghent, E. (1989). Credo. *Contemporary Psychoanalysis* 25:169–211.

Giovacchini, P. (1975). *Psychoanalysis of Character Disorders.* New York: Jason Aronson.

Greenberg, J. R. (1986). Theoretical models and the analyst's neutrality. *Contemporary Psychoanalysis* 22:87–106.

Greenson, R. (1967). *The Technique and Practice of Psychoanalysis.* New York: International Universities Press.

_______ (1968). Disidentifying from mother: its special importance for the boy. In *Explorations in Psychoanalysis,* pp. 305–312. New York: International Universities Press, 1978.

_______ (1969). The origin and fate of new ideas. In *Explorations in Psychoanalysis,* pp. 171–190. New York: International Universities Press, 1978.

_______ (1971). The nontransference relationship in the psychoanalytic situation. In *Explorations in Psychoanalysis,* pp. 359–386. New York: International Universities Press, 1978.

_______ (1974). Loving, hating and indifference towards the patient. *International Review of Psycho-Analysis* 1:259–266.

Grotstein, J. (1990). Nothingness, meaninglessness, chaos, and the "black hole." I. In *Contemporary Psychoanalysis* 26:257–290.

Grunes, M. (1984). The therapeutic object relationship. *Psychoanalytic Review* 71:123–143.

Guntrip, H. (1971). The schizoid problem. In *Psychoanalytic Theory, Therapy, and the Self,* pp. 145–173. New York: Basic Books.

______ (1975). My experience of analysis with Fairbairn and Winnicott. *International Review of Psycho-Analysis* 2:145–156.

Hartmann, H. (1939). *Ego Psychology and the Problem of Adaptation.* New York: International Universities Press, 1958.

Hirsch, I. (1987). Varying modes of analytic participation. *Journal of the American Academy of Psychoanalysis* 15:205–222.

Horner, A. (1984). *Object Relations and the Developing Ego in Therapy.* 2nd ed. New York: Jason Aronson

______ ed. (1985). *Treating the Oedipal Patient in Brief Psychotherapy.* New York: Jason Aronson.

______ (1987). The "real" relationship and analytic neutrality. *Journal of the American Academy of Psychoanalysis* 15:491–501.

______ (1988). The constructed self and developmental discontinuity. *Journal of the American Academy of Psychoanalysis* 16:235–238.

______ (1989). *The Wish for Power and the Fear of Having It.* Northvale, NJ: Jason Aronson.

______ (1990). *Being and Loving.* 3rd ed. Northvale, NJ: Jason Aronson.

______ (1991a) Money issues and analytic neutrality. In *Money and Mind,* ed. S. Klebanow and E. Lowenkopf, pp. 175–182. New York: Plenum.

______ (1991b). *The Primacy of Structure: The Psychotherapy of Underlying Character Pathology.* Northvale, NJ: Jason Aronson.

Horowitz, M. (1990). A model of mourning: change in schemas of self and other. *Journal of the American Psychoanalytic Association* 38:297–324.

Ingram, D. (1987). *Horney's theory of psychoanalytic technique and traditional modes of therapeutic intervention.* Presented at The William Alanson White Society Meeting, New York (unpublished).

Jacobson, E. (1964). *The Self and the Object World.* New York: International Universities Press.

Joseph, B. (1985). Transference: the total situation. *International Journal of Psycho-Analysis* 66:447–454.

Kavanagh, G. (1985). Changes in the patient's object representations during psychoanalysis and psychoanalytic psychotherapy. *Bulletin of the Menninger Clinic* 49:546–564.

Kernberg, O. (1965). Notes on countertransference. *Journal of the American Psychoanalytic Association* 13:38–56.

______ (1976). *Object Relations Theory and Clinical Psychoanalysis.* New York: Jason Aronson.

______ (1980). *Internal World and External Reality.* New York: Jason Aronson.

______ (1986). Projection and projective identification: developmental and clinical aspects. *Journal of the American Psychoanalytic Association Monograph,* pp. 795–819.

______ (1987). An ego psychology–object relations theory approach to the transference. *Psychoanalytic Quarterly* 56:197–221.

Kernberg, O., Selzer, M., Koenigsberg, H., Carr, A., and Appelbaum, A. (1989). *Psychodynamic Psychotherapy of Borderline Patients.* New York: Basic Books.

Khan, M. M. R. (1963). The concept of cumulative trauma. *Psychoanalytic Study of the Child* 18:286–306. New York: International Universities Press.

Kirkpatrick, M. (1990). Thoughts about the origins of femininity. *Journal of the American Academy of Psychoanalysis* 18:554–565.

Klein, M. (1959). Our adult world and its roots in infancy. In *Envy and Gratitude and Other Works,* pp. 247–263. New York: Delacorte.

Kohut, H. (1971). *The Analysis of the Self.* New York: International Universities Press.

______ (1977). *The Restoration of the Self.* New York: International Universities Press.

______ (1984). *How Does Analysis Cure?* Chicago, IL: University of Chicago Press.

Krystal, H. (1978). Trauma and affect. *Psychoanalytic Study of the Child* 33:81–116. New Haven, CT: Yale University Press.

Kubie, L. S. (1950). *Practical and Theoretical Aspects of Psychoanalysis.* New York: International Universities Press.

Langs, R. (1974). *The Technique of Psychoanalytic Psychotherapy.* Vol. 2. New York: Jason Aronson.

______ (1979a). *The Therapeutic Environment.* New York: Jason Aronson.

______ (1979b). Interventions in the bipersonal field. *Contemporary Psychoanalysis* 15:1–54.

Levy, S. (1985). Empathy and psychoanalytic technique. *Journal of the American Psychoanalytic Association* 33:353–378.

Lichtenberg, J. D. (1975). The development of a sense of self. *Journal of the American Psychoanalytic Association* 23:453–484.

Little, M. (1990). *Psychotic Anxieties and Containment.* Northvale, NJ: Jason Aronson.

Loewald, H. (1979). The waning of the Oedipus complex. *Journal of the American Psychoanalytic Association* 27:751–775.

______ (1985). Oedipus complex and the development of self. *Psychoanalytic Quarterly* 54:435–443.

——— (1986). Transference–countertransference. *Journal of the American Psychoanalytic Association* 34:275–288.

Luborsky, L., Crits-Christoph, P., Mintz, J., and Auerbach, A. (1988). *Who Will Benefit from Psychotherapy? Predicting Therapeutic Outcomes.* New York: Basic Books.

Mahler, M. (1968). *On Human Symbiosis and the Vicissitudes of Individuation.* New York: International Universities Press.

Mahler, M., Pine, F., and Bergman, A. (1975). *The Psychological Birth of the Human Infant.* New York: Basic Books.

Mann, J. (1973a). Confrontation as a mode of teaching. In *Confrontation in Psychotherapy,* ed. G. Adler and P. Myerson, pp. 23–37. New York: Science House.

——— (1973b). *Time-Limited Psychotherapy.* Cambridge, MA: Harvard University Press.

Maturana, H. R., and Varela, F. J. (1987). *The Tree of Knowledge.* Boston, MA: Shambhala.

Mitchell, S. (1986). The wings of Icarus: illusion and the problem of narcissism. *Contemporary Psychoanalysis* 22:107–132.

Modell, A. (1991). The therapeutic relationship as a paradoxical experience. *Psychoanalytic Dialogues* 1:13–28.

Nemiah, J. C. (1978). Alexithymia and psychosomatic illness. *Journal of Continuing Education in Psychiatry* 39:25–37.

Paolino, T. (1982). The therapeutic relationship in psychoanalysis. *Contemporary Psychoanalysis* 18:218–234.

Piaget, J. (1936). *The Origins of Intelligence in Children.* New York: International Universities Press, 1952.

Pine, F. (1979). On the pathology of the separation-individuation process as manifested in later clinical work. *International Journal of Psycho-Analysis* 60:225–242.

Poland, W. (1984). On the analyst's neutrality. *Journal of the American Psychoanalytic Association* 32:284–299.

Racker, H. (1968). *Transference and Countertransference.* New York: International Universities Press.

Rose, G. (1974). Some misuses of analysis as a way of life: analysis interminable and interminable "analysts." *International Review of Psycho-Analysis* 1:509–515.

Rutter, M. (1974). *The Qualities of Mothering: Maternal Deprivation Reassessed*. New York: Jason Aronson.

Sandler, A. M. (1975). On the significance of Piaget's work for psychoanalysis. *International Review of Psycho-Analysis* 2:365–377.

Sandler, J. (1981). Unconscious wishes and human relationships. *Contemporary Psychoanalysis* 17:180–196.

______ (1990). On internal object relations. *Journal of the American Psychoanalytic Association* 38:859–880.

Schafer, R. (1960). The loving and beloved superego in Freud's structural theory. *Psychoanalytic Study of the Child* 15:163–199. New York: International Universities Press.

______ (1983). *The Analytic Attitude*. New York: Basic Books.

Scharff, D., and Scharff, J. (1989). *Object Relations Family Therapy*. Northvale, NJ: Jason Aronson.

______ (1991). *Object Relations Couple Therapy*. Northvale, NJ: Jason Aronson.

Schechter, D. (1968). Identification and individuation. *Journal of the American Psychoanalytic Association* 18:48–80.

Schubart, W. (1989). The patient in the psychoanalyst's consulting room—the first consultation as a psychoanalytic encounter. *International Journal of Psycho-Analysis* 70:423–432.

Segal, H. (1982). Early infantile development as reflected in the psychoanalytical process: steps in integration. *International Journal of Psycho-Analysis* 63:15–22.

Shapiro, R. (1990). Modulating phenomena: elusive aspects of the psychoanalytic process. *Contemporary Psychoanalysis* 26:497–517.

Shapiro, T. (1989). Editorial: our changing science. *Journal of the American Psychoanalytic Association* 37:3–6.

Slipp, S. (1973). The symbiotic survival pattern: a relational theory of schizophrenia. *Family Process* 12:377–397.

——— (1984). *Object Relations: A Dynamic Bridge Between Individual and Family Treatment.* Northvale, NJ: Jason Aronson.

Stern, D. (1985). *The Interpersonal World of the Infant: A View from Psychoanalysis and Developmental Psychology.* New York: Basic Books

Strachey, J. (1957). Editor's note. In *Abstracts of the Standard Edition of the Complete Psychological Works of Sigmund Freud* 14:164. London: Hogarth Press.

Sullivan, H. S. (1940). *Conceptions of Modern Psychiatry.* New York: Norton.

Tansey, M. and Burke, W. (1989). *Understanding Countertransference: From Projective Identification to Empathy.* Hillsdale, NJ: The Analytic Press.

Wachtel, P. (1986). On the limits of therapeutic neutrality. *Contemporary Psychoanalysis* 22:60–70.

Watzlawick, P., Beavin, J., and Jackson, D. (1967). *The Pragmatics of Human Communication.* New York: Norton.

Winnicott, D. W. (1951). Transitional objects and transitional phenomena. In *Through Pediatrics to Psychoanalysis,* pp. 229–242. New York: Basic Books, 1975.

——— (1960a). The theory of the parent–infant relationship. In *The Maturational Processes and the Facilitating Environment,* pp. 37–55. New York: International Universities Press, 1965.

——— (1960b). Ego distortion in terms of true and false self. In *The Maturational Processes and the Facilitating Environment,* pp. 140–152. New York: International Universities Press, 1965.

——— (1965). *The Maturational Processes and the Facilitating Environment.* New York: International Universities Press.

——— (1975). Fear of breakdown. *International Review of Psycho-Analysis* 1:103–107.

Zetzel, E. (1965). The theory of therapy in relation to a developmental model of the psychic apparatus. *International Journal of Psycho-Analysis* 46:39–52.

# Index